ENGLISH CATHEDRALS

The Prior's Door at Ely, one of the three surviving doorways of the former cloisters. Its simple but moving tympanum was carved in about 1140.

ENGLISH CATHEDRALS

PATRICK CORMACK

THE ENGLISH TOURIST BOARD

WEIDENFELD AND NICOLSON   LONDON

To my mother

Above : A gilded roof boss at Lichfield.

*Endpapers : Pools of multi-coloured light, filtered through stained glass,
dapple the floor at Gloucester Cathedral.*

First published in Great Britain by
George Weidenfeld and Nicolson Limited
91 Clapham High Street, London sw4 7TA

ISBN 0 297 78414 5

Picture research by Cathy Ellis
Design by Joyce Chester and Sheila Sherwen
Filmset by Keyspools Limited, Golborne, Lancashire
Printed and bound in Italy by LEGO, Vicenza

CONTENTS

The exquisite fan vault in the great central tower at Canterbury known as Bell Harry.

FOREWORD BY SIR HUGH CASSON

President of the Royal Academy

Some twenty million people each year visit the forty-two Anglican cathedrals of England. They come either to worship or to admire. Many of them are tourists – a high proportion foreign – and since, like their predecessors the pilgrims, so many come from far away they take their visit seriously. Postcards are bought, guides consulted, cameras clicked. What do they look for? Beauty and mystery of course, but also a sense of order and space, an awareness of the continuity of time. What do they see? Noble architecture, lively sculpture, rich glass, fine plate and vestments, relics for the most part of the time when the Church dominated totally the lives of men, just as its towers and spires still command our towns and villages. Such visual wealth can be bewildering in its variety and style, and most of us know that really to enjoy it, it is necessary to understand it, to know a little at least of how, why and by whom these masterpieces were built and adorned.

It is the purpose of this richly packed handbook to meet this need by providing in simple and concise form a series of portraits, lightly delineated and easy to compare each with the other. Together they form an admirable and perceptive record of what is there and why. I am sure it will be widely welcomed as a treasured companion for all those planning to visit, or re-visit, some of the finest buildings in the world – the cathedrals of England.

Hugh Casson
London 1984

PREFACE

This short book attempts to give some idea of the beauty and majesty of the cathedrals of the Church of England, one of the finest and best preserved groups of great buildings in the world. Among them are the jewels of Britain's architectural heritage.

It does not seek to rival or replace the notable works of scholarship by such authorities as John Harvey and Alec Clifton Taylor, but surprisingly few books have sought to deal with each of these great cathedrals separately and I hope that this approach will be helpful, particularly to those who are planning their first visits. What I have sought to do is to give an impression of the personality of each cathedral (and no two are alike), to convey the atmosphere as well as to recount the most significant events in its history, and to describe its principal features and major treasures. I hope I will succeed in whetting the appetites of those to whom these buildings are unknown, and in reviving treasured memories in those to whom they are familiar.

Essentially this is a book about England's medieval cathedrals but there are forty-two dioceses in the country, and medieval cathedrals, and the Renaissance St Paul's, serve only twenty-six of them. For the sake of completeness, therefore, I have added brief chapters on the four 'purpose-built' cathedrals erected during the last hundred years and another on the former parish churches which serve as the cathedrals for a dozen of the newer dioceses.

If there are mistakes or blemishes the fault is mine but I would like to thank all those who have helped me with this book, in particular those deans and provosts who have taken an interest in the project; Sir Hugh Casson, President of the Royal Academy, for so generously agreeing to write the Foreword; Sebastian Wilberforce who helped me to assemble some of the vast number of books and pamphlets on the subject; Wendy Dallas of Weidenfeld & Nicolson who was, as always, unfailingly helpful and patient; Cathy Ellis, also of Weidenfeld and Nicolson, for doing the picture research; and finally my splendid secretary June Sharman and my wife Mary who, working as usual to an impossible deadline, typed the manuscript without either assaulting the author, or losing their sense of humour.

Patrick Cormack
Enville,
Staffordshire

INTRODUCTION: THE CATHEDRALS OF ENGLAND

The cathedrals of the medieval period are England's greatest public buildings. Built to express, through great art and craftsmanship, man's love of God, and to be fitting centres for the dioceses they served, they were, until the coming of the railway age, England's largest public buildings as well. Still of enormous spiritual significance to all Christians, they have an importance far beyond the religious. As supreme works of art and the homes of priceless treasures, every year they attract millions of visitors, of all faiths and of none.

There are, of course, many important and noble churches in England which are not cathedrals. Some, like Tewkesbury Abbey or Beverley Minster, never were cathedrals; others, like Bath and Westminster Abbey, once were. The essential definition of a cathedral, the feature which separates it from every other church, is that it contains the cathedra, or throne, of the bishop of the diocese.

England was divided into these areas of ecclesiastical jurisdiction long before the Conquest. Indeed, by 1066 there were sixteen dioceses in England, of which all but five (Elmham in East Anglia, Selsey on the south coast, Sherborne in Dorset, Ramsbury in Wiltshire, and Dorchester in Oxfordshire) survive. Of these first Saxon cathedrals, however, little is known. Most were built of wood and, like the earliest Christian churches on the Continent, were doubtless modelled on the basilica, or public hall, found in every Roman town. There, from a raised dais at the end of the hall the magistrate would dispense justice. In the early church the dais end became the apse, and there the bishop's chair was placed – a position it occupies today only in Norwich.

After the Conquest the ecclesiastical map of England was partly redrawn to ensure that every cathedral was in a town of major importance. Dorchester was replaced by Lincoln; Selsey by Chichester; Ramsbury first by Old Sarum and then by Salisbury, which also absorbed the diocese of Sherborne; and Elmham moved to Thetford and then to Norwich. In 1109 the diocese of Ely was created, and in 1133 Carlisle. These were the pre-Reformation dioceses of England and it was because they were so few and so large that their mother churches, unlike many of the multitude of provincial cathedrals in Italy and France, became so grand and glorious. True centres of pilgrimage and devotion, they were also objects of regional generosity, provoked either by genuine devotion or by a desire to compensate for the sins of this world and so ease the passage into the next.

With the Reformation the ecclesiastical map of England was further subdivided when Henry VIII made a number of great abbey churches, whose monasteries he had dissolved, into cathedrals: Gloucester, Peterborough, Bristol, Chester, Oxford and, very briefly, Westminster – a cathedral for only ten years.

No new dioceses were created between 1546 and 1836 but between then and 1927 their number almost doubled and today there are forty-two dioceses in the Church of England. Only four of the newer cathedrals, however, are notable medieval churches: Ripon (1836); St Albans (1878); Southwell (1884); and Southwark (1905). There are thus twenty-five major medieval cathedrals and one – St Paul's, seat of the Bishop of London – glorious Renaissance one. Christopher Wren's masterpiece was built because the Fire of London in 1666 destroyed Old St Paul's, at that time one of the two largest churches in Christendom.

During the last century four cathedrals have been built to serve new dioceses. Truro is the only cathedral built by the Victorians. Coventry is a post-war building, built to replace the promoted parish church cathedral which was destroyed in 1940. Guildford was begun in 1936 but completed between 1952 and 1965. And the enormous Anglican cathedral at Liverpool was begun in 1904 and finished in 1978. England's other twelve most recently created cathedrals are all former parish churches, upgraded to serve new dioceses carved out of the old to meet the pressures of a rising population: Birmingham, Blackburn, Bradford,

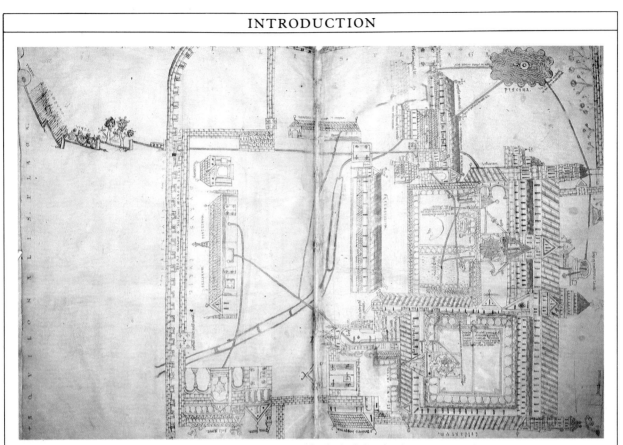

*A twelfth-century plan of Canterbury Cathedral showing its monastic buildings
and its fresh water system.*

Chelmsford, Derby, St Edmundsbury, Leicester, Manchester, Newcastle, Portsmouth, Sheffield and Wakefield.

Although it seeks to say something about the new ones and to pick out the most notable features of the twelve just mentioned, this book is essentially about the twenty-six great cathedrals. Something will be said about how they were built in the next chapter, but one very special feature must be mentioned here. Unlike almost all the Continental cathedrals, seven of the seventeen cathedrals in England in the Middle Ages were also abbey churches of great Benedictine monasteries, of which the bishop was the abbot: Canterbury, Rochester, Winchester, Worcester, Durham, Norwich and Ely. Bath, which served intermittently as the sole or joint cathedral of Somerset for the whole of the twelfth century, was also a Benedictine house, and four more (Peterborough, Gloucester, Chester and Westminister) were given cathedral status by Henry VIII.

The other medieval cathedrals were served by canons. Carlisle was an Augustinian house and was therefore regarded as a monastery because the Augustinian, or Austin, canons lived according to a strict rule or 'regula'. These Canons Regular as they were known, controlled some two hundred English abbeys and priories and two more of their great abbey churches, at Bristol and at Oxford, became cathedrals after the dissolution of the monasteries.

The other cathedrals of medieval England were served by secular canons. These clergy followed no prescribed rule of life and derived their income from the ownership of land, endowments which were known as prebends. Those who held these prebends were known as prebendaries, and they formed the body known as the Chapter which was responsible for administering the cathedral's affairs.

Those cathedrals always run by secular (or non-monastic) clergy have been referred to since the Reformation as cathedrals of the Old Foundation: London, York, Lichfield, Hereford, Exeter (all pre-Conquest foundations), and Lincoln, Chichester,

Wells and Salisbury. When he dissolved the monasteries Henry VIII refounded the monastic cathedrals and these, together with the new cathedrals he created, are known as the cathedrals of the New Foundation.

Their construction and their use

How were they built, these great churches, large enough to hold the whole Christian population of a city, and expressing in their structure and adornments man's supreme creative skill, harnessed to glorify his creator? We marvel at their form and beauty. Equally worthy of wonder and praise are the techniques and organization that made them possible, and which knit together successive bands of masons, carpenters, glaziers and others, often over many generations. Although only two great English cathedrals (Durham and Salisbury) were largely completed within a life span, cathedrals fared better here than many on the Continent. Cologne was not finished until 1880 and Beauvais was never completed. Even so, Bristol was without a nave for four hundred years, and the building of Liverpool has taken almost the whole of the present century.

It is hardly surprising that we have little documentary evidence of precisely how medieval cathedrals were built. We do, however, have the account by Gervase, a monastic chronicler, of the rebuilding of the choir at Canterbury after a disastrous fire in 1174. He records the process of construction in detail, telling us how the monks, shortly after the fire on 5 September, called in artists to seek their advice. Little changes. It is rather like an account of a local authority putting out its work to tender. There were even debates as to whether the best method of proceeding was to restore and adapt the ruins, or pull them down and start again. The monks of Canterbury were fortunate in their choice of architect. They commissioned William of Sens and Gervase tells us how he won the monks' confidence, assembled a team of masons around him, sent for stone from Normandy, and arranged for its transportation and its cutting. Within five years of the fire he had finished the western part of a completely new choir and of the transept behind it. His work is rightly regarded as a landmark in the history of cathedral building. Sadly, he fell and injured himself badly when some scaffolding from which he was supervising the work gave way, but his design was sufficiently advanced for another notable master, William the Englishman, to finish it.

In Gervase's account we can see how the team worked together: the abbey community who commissioned the work, the master mason who was the architect, and the artists and craftsmen he assembled. From this narrative, from the account of York in the fourteenth century, and from the research of modern scholars (especially the great architectural historian John Harvey), we can piece together something of how a cathedral was built, of how problems were surmounted by men who knew nothing of the sophisticated gadgetry we take for granted. However, as John Harvey points out, the actual process of building did not change very much from the beginning of the twelfth century to the beginning of the nineteenth. He goes so far as to say that there was 'a closer link between the methods of, say, 1125 and 1925 than between those of 1925 and 1950'. It all underlines the rather sad fact that today it is only among the craftsmen who are concerned with the maintenance and repair of the great buildings of the past that one can find any continuity with the traditional skills and crafts.

Once a decision to build a cathedral had been taken, the first thing to be done was to transfer the design prepared by the master mason to the ground. The building would probably be orientated by making an alignment that corresponded with sunrise on the patronal festival. The researches of the Reverend Hugh Benson have shown, for instance, that the orientation of Oxford Cathedral was to sunrise on Lady Day, 25 March, in the eighth century, while Rochester points precisely to sunrise on 30 November, St Andrew's Day, at the end of the eleventh century.

The design approved and the site pegged out, the foundation trenches were dug, and generally filled with stone rubble pressed firmly down, though where the ground was marshy piles would be driven and then stones placed on stout timbers.

To determine height, rods would be marked to the appropriate levels and plumb-lines used to ensure that the walls were truly vertical. This was an exercise that called for total accuracy, for the roof and vault had to be sprung from the walls. It is very probable that three-dimensional models were made, but none has survived earlier than a fifteenth-century one in Rouen. We do, however, have Sir Christopher Wren's magnificent model of St Paul's which indicates the sort of thing that his predecessors might have constructed. Though medieval architects appear to have known nothing of solid

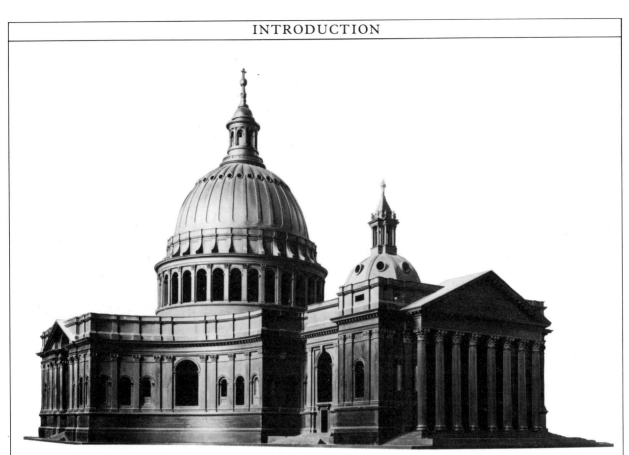

The wooden model Christopher Wren constructed and which shows his first design for St Paul's Cathedral. It is on view in the crypt.

geometry, we do know that the ground plan was probably based on a grid of lines in squares of 10, 25, 50 or 100 feet. We know too that on occasions there were in effect dress rehearsals for building, as when the timbers that formed the roof of Westminster Hall at the end of the fourteenth century were laid out on the ground at Farnham before being brought to Westminster and erected. We know that craftsmen were so carefully and professionally organized by the middle of the fourteenth century that there was a special drawing office for those who were working on the cathedral at York. The office still survives, but of the drawings that those draughtsmen produced we know nothing. It is hardly surprising that working documents generally perished (though there are a few examples in various parts of Europe, some in Strasburg for instance and a fairly major collection in Vienna) but it is not only the very perishable nature of the drawings that explains why there is virtually no evidence of precise methods. Much of the information that masons used was a closely guarded secret among themselves, which they did not want others to share. Even then

there were fraternities, trade secrets – and closed shops. But each mason had his special mark and we can trace the progress, even if we do not know the names, of some who worked on several churches.

One of the biggest problems the builders faced was finding adequate supplies of timber and stone. The timber was needed not only for roofs and other parts of the building, but for the scaffolding essential to its erection. Sometimes whole tracts of forest would be bought up and often intensive searches had to be undertaken to find precisely the right type of trees for a specific purpose. There is a splendid story that Abbot Suger, of the Abbey of S. Denis in Paris, angrily refuted those who told him that the timbers he needed were not available and went out to search the forest himself until he found what was needed. We have only to look at the lantern of Ely Cathedral, depending, as it does, on eight massive oak trees for support, to realize how essential it was to have adequate supplies of particular species of trees, as well as the vast quantities of wood needed for scaffolding and for the shelters necessary to protect unfinished work from November until

March, and for making machinery to load and unload stone.

As for quarries, much of the stone used in the southern cathedrals of England came from Caen in Normandy, a journey which was helped by the fact that, until King John carelessly lost it, Normandy was linked to the English crown. In England itself the quarries of the great limestone belt were exploited. The most famous were those at Barnack, which were used for Peterborough Cathedral, and Doulting, the quarry for Wells. Where there was no limestone, sandstone was often the choice, as at Lichfield, Carlisle and the great abbey church at Chester, which became a cathedral in 1554.

The stone would be prised away from the quarries by driving massive wooden wedges into natural cracks, a cumbersome process which shows why large stones were, at least until the end of the twelfth century, rarely used except to provide corner stones, doors and windows. Even much later the centres of walls and pillars were often filled with stone rubble from the fields. Iron, too, was extensively used to strengthen and sustain. Few people who visit Westminster Abbey realize that the iron tie bars have been there as long as the arches they support.

Conscious of the problems caused if sufficient time was not allowed for the walls to settle, the medieval master mason would rarely build more than ten feet vertically during the season, which lasted from 1 March to the end of October. There were other enemies to contend with too during construction, especially wind and fire, and then when the building was complete the elements would immediately begin the long and inevitable process of erosion. That is why so often medieval buildings were given an annual coat of protective whitewash. Perhaps the most famous example of this was the great main tower at the Tower of London. It came to be known as the White Tower as a result.

To protect the building further the rain was funnelled off the roof. Special spouts were designed, which would spew the water away from the walls, hence the often elaborately carved gargoyles which grin down on us still. It is interesting to note that much of the carving both inside and outside cathedrals was for the ingenious covering up of some functional contrivance.

Essential to the stability of the structure was the achievement of a proper balance, that counterplay of thrusts of arches, vaults and buttresses. In all this, nothing was of more importance than the vaulting.

A model of the octagon at Ely – one of the architectural wonders of the medieval age.

To describe the theory behind the construction of these often elaborately beautiful coverings is to run the risk of over-simplification, but though techniques improved to the point where the shell of a vault might be as thin as six inches or even less, the principles of construction remained similar from the eleventh to the fifteenth century.

The roof timbers were lifted by means of a windlass (there are medieval examples surviving at Peterborough, Salisbury and Beverley) and a wheel. Operated by two men walking within it, the wheel would be capable of raising huge loads a hundred feet or more above the ground. The wooden centrings would then be installed on the scaffolding to support the arched stone ribs until the mortar was set. These ribs would carry the webbing which was, in effect, the roof itself. Working one bay at a time the masons would hoist the stones of the ribs (the voussoirs) on to the centring and mortar them into place. Then a keystone would be inserted to lock the ribs together. This would eventually form a finely carved and painted boss. Later a layer of concrete would be poured over the vault and then the masons would move to the next bay to repeat the process. In many vaults the ribs are not all structural. They were merely added for the purposes of enrichment and adornment. We can see this at Exeter. The thirteenth-century choir vaulting has structural ribs, whilst those in the fourteenth-century nave are purely decorative.

In our proper admiration for the skill of the medieval builders we should not forget that they, as did their castle-building colleagues, owed much to what was observed and learnt from the Moors by those who went on the Crusades. Nor should we imagine that everything was sweetness and light on a medieval building site. There are disturbingly familiar graphic accounts from mid-fourteenth-century York of strikes and pilfering. Nothing, however, can disguise the fact that the building of a great cathedral was a sublime achievement. At the centre of all was the master mason who was, in effect, the architect. Largely owing to the researches of John Harvey we know the identity of most of those who worked on our great cathedrals. William of Sens at Canterbury, Richard Walbaston at Durham, Richard of Gainsborough at Lincoln, and – above all – the great Henry Yevele at Westminster and Canterbury are now rightly regarded as among the foremost architects of all time.

Without money, however, nothing could have been achieved. Many of the ways in which the building of medieval cathedrals was financed were entirely of their time, such as the sale of indulgences (a written papal guarantee that sins were forgiven) and the gifts of rich prelates grown fat on the Church's vast estates. Important, too, were the wealthy merchants who gave not just to show influence but to buy glory, they hoped, for all eternity. There were Guilds of Benefactors who came together to raise money from the townsfolk and the thank-offerings of those who had recovered from illness following a visit to a shrine. To these sums were added the proceeds of alms boxes and the money taken from people who sought admission to the shrines. Modern fund-raisers employ some of the same techniques.

No matter how mercenary, and even questionable, some of these methods of fund-raising may seem, nothing should blind us to the fact that the cathedrals were built to the glory of God. Their very structure, with spires and arches pointing to the heavens, was part of that grand symbolism echoed by Wren in the seventeenth century when he built the great dome of St Paul's, a replica of heaven itself.

Cathedrals were built, too, for regular worship. This is something we easily forget today unless perhaps we happen to be present at daily Evensong. In medieval times seven canonical hours were sung every day, and the monastic custom was to divide the twenty-four hours of the day into twelve night hours and twelve day hours, with Matins generally said in the middle of the night. Times were regulated by the hours of daylight, so that in the winter months the monks would go to bed at seven and rise twelve hours later, having interrupted their sleep for Matins in the middle. In the shorter summer night there was little time for sleep, and that was why in 1548 midnight Matins were abolished by a royal injunction which ordered that they should be sung at 6 a.m. instead.

The choir was the setting for the daily offices but on Sundays there would be a procession round the whole church. Leaving the choir it would turn up the north aisle and encircle choir and altar, making its station before the great cross or rood which would inevitably dominate the nave. When he made his will in 1445 the Bishop of Lincoln asked that he should be buried in the place where he had stood in that procession. Processions in monastic cathedrals were more elaborate ceremonies than those in secular ones for they included a tour not only of all the altars of the church but of the principal buildings of the cloister as well.

When the feast day of a saint to whom an altar in the church was dedicated fell on a Sunday the procession would begin by visiting that altar, and there were always special arrangements on feast days. Then the festal procession would be headed by a clerk bearing and sprinkling holy water, followed by three more, resplendent in copes and carrying three crosses side by side. Next would come two clerks in albs, bearing candlesticks, and behind them incense bearers, and then clerks bearing the sacred relics. Then would come the sub-deacon with the Book of the Gospels, followed by the processional cross and, finally, by the celebrant attended by servers in copes.

It was for such solemn and resplendent pageantry that these great churches were built. It is fitting that today they should still be the setting for the most dignified ritual, and the guardians of the best music, which the Church can offer.

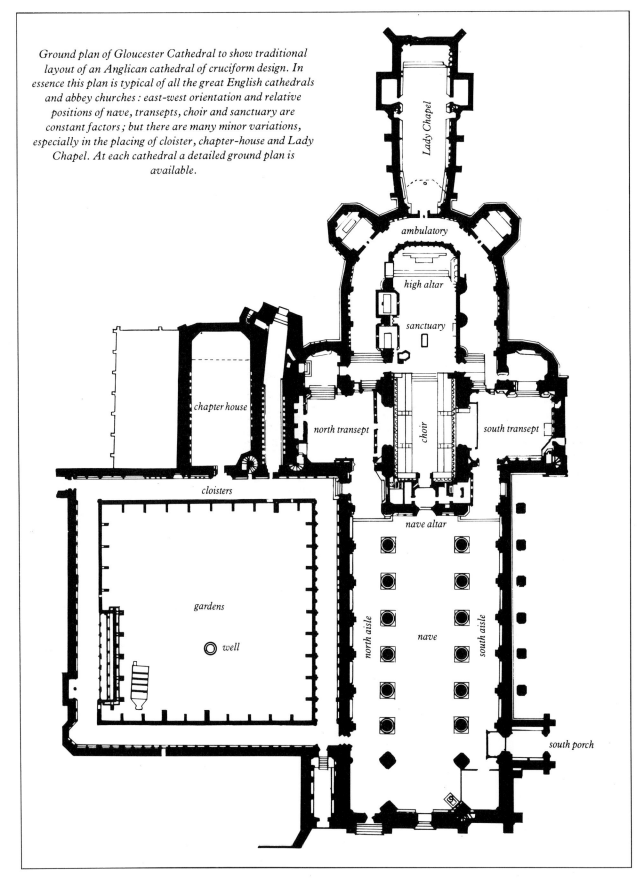

Ground plan of Gloucester Cathedral to show traditional layout of an Anglican cathedral of cruciform design. In essence this plan is typical of all the great English cathedrals and abbey churches : east-west orientation and relative positions of nave, transepts, choir and sanctuary are constant factors ; but there are many minor variations, especially in the placing of cloister, chapter-house and Lady Chapel. At each cathedral a detailed ground plan is available.

Lady Chapel

ambulatory

high altar

sanctuary

chapter house

north transept

choir

south transept

cloisters

nave altar

gardens

well

north aisle

nave

south aisle

south porch

ARCHITECTURAL STYLES

A note on the principal styles of English architecture referred to in the text

Norman or Romanesque (1066–1200)
A style characterized by massive masonry and heavy proportions, round arches, and barrel, groined, and – finally – ribbed vaulting.

Early English (1175–1270)
The first phase of English Gothic, it is recognizable by its lancet windows and, later, its geometrical tracery. The emphasis throughout is on thin linear articulation rather than on mass and volume.

Decorated (1250–1370)
The Decorated style was characterized by elaborate curvilinear tracery, complicated rib vaulting, cusping and naturalistic carving, especially of foliage.

Perpendicular (1340–1550)
The last phase of English Gothic architecture, it is typified by light, airy proportions, straight lattice-like tracery over windows and wall surfaces, shallow mouldings, four-centred arches and fan vaults.

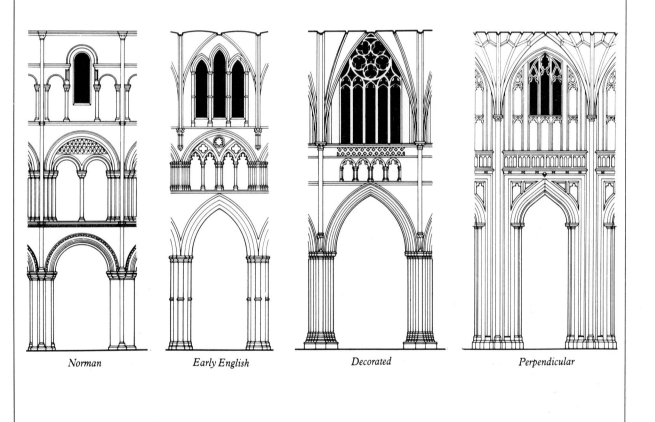

Norman *Early English* *Decorated* *Perpendicular*

PRE-REFORMATION CATHEDRALS

CANTERBURY

The Cathedral Church of Christ

For an English man or woman with a sense of history the first visit to Canterbury is still in a sense journey's end, for in this cradle of English Christianity lies what was for centuries one of the greatest centres of pilgrimage in Christendom, the shrine of the man who, far more than the mythical dragon-slayer, was England's patron saint. I can never come here without thinking of this, and of those generations of medieval pilgrims described by Chaucer as they cantered here in that April springtime six centuries ago, 'the holy blissful martyr for to seke'.

Before the pilgrims came Augustine, and after them Erasmus. The prophet of the new learning was dazzled and awed, in spite of himself, by Becket's shrine and it has always been a place of special significance for Christians. Three centuries ago the persecuted Protestants of France were given refuge here to conduct their worship in a chapel which their descendants still use, and in 1982 Pope John Paul II, successor of the sixth-century Pope Gregory the Great, came here to meet Augustine's successor, Archbishop Robert Runcie – a unique moment in the history of the Church of England and also of the Church *in* England.

Though Gregory thought that English Christians would be governed from missionary centres in London and York, it was to Canterbury that Augustine first came in 597 with his forty Benedictine monks, and it was here that King Ethelbert was baptized on Whit Sunday in that year. And under the King's protection Augustine established his cathedral. Ever since then, Canterbury, in spite of challenges from York, has been reckoned the first in precedence among the cathedral churches of England, a precedence reluctantly conceded by the first Norman Archbishop of York and finally and unequivocally established in 1352, when the Pope laid it down that Canterbury's archbishop should be Primate of All England: a supremacy that is still most tangibly and graphically expressed at every coronation service, when it is the Archbishop of Canterbury who places the crown upon the sovereign's head.

A detail of the Becket window in the north aisle, the only surviving twelfth-century 'portrait' of the saint.

*From the south-east, as pilgrims have seen it
for five centuries.*

If all that we had here was a cathedral reconstructed by the Victorians or rebuilt more recently on an ancient site, this would still be hallowed ground, but mercifully we can still see Canterbury much as Chaucer's pilgrims saw it, though more beautiful by far than it was then, for it is crowned by the most perfect Perpendicular tower in England, built a hundred years after Chaucer's time. Inside, though the shrine has gone, we can still follow the pilgrims' way, climbing as they did to the site of the tomb and we can still see, in some of the most beautiful painted glass in Europe, a representation of Becket by an artist who might well have known him.

Nothing remains of the early Saxon cathedral, though by the time William the Conqueror came Canterbury already housed the remains of some of the greatest of the Saxons: Odo, Dunstan, Alphage, and other great and saintly archbishops who helped make Canterbury not only a place of prayer but a place of learning. William the Conqueror dispossessed and imprisoned Stigand, the last of the Saxon archbishops, but by the time he appointed Lanfranc in 1070 the Saxon cathedral had been destroyed by the great fire of 1067.

Lanfranc was seventy but he was a man of prodigious energy as well as real piety. He founded the monastery of Christ Church and set about rebuilding the cathedral. By the time he died, in 1093, there were over a hundred monks at Canterbury, but only the merest fragments of his cathedral remain. Building was energetically carried on by his successor, Anselm, and when he died in 1109 the great Norman crypt, undoubtedly the finest of English cathedral crypts, was complete.

It was the last thirty years of the twelfth century which were the most crucial in the history of this great building, for the tragedy and calamity which occurred in quick succession inspired the determination and provided the opportunity to make this place a worthy shrine and mother church of England.

First came the tragedy of 1170. In 1162 Henry II had appointed his Chancellor and boon companion, Thomas à Becket, as Archbishop of Canterbury, though he was then only a deacon. Becket now felt that he had a new and greater master to serve than the king who had promoted him. The next eight years were years of conflict and quarrel between king and prelate over the position and importance of the Church and its law. For a time Becket was exiled and although there was a reconciliation in 1170 it was but a brief affair. Then Henry is reputed to have uttered the famous words, 'Who will rid me of this turbulent priest?' Four knights, William de Tracey, Reginald Fitzurse, Richard le Breton and Hugh de Morville, saw it as a challenge that could bring them glory. They sailed across the Channel and on 29 December 1170 came to Canterbury, where Becket was prepared for, and almost seemed to welcome, the prospect of martyrdom. The story is most brilliantly told in one of the twentieth century's finest plays, T. S. Eliot's *Murder in the Cathedral*.

The choir raised high above its crypt, looking east towards
the Trinity Chapel and the Corona.

Struck down at the altar, Becket was proclaimed a martyr and almost immediately miracles were reported at his tomb. The King himself came to do penance and Canterbury attained European importance as a centre of pilgrimage when Becket was canonized in 1173.

It is to this terrible crime and the repercussions it had throughout Christendom that we owe the form of the present cathedral – to this and also to the fire of 1174 when, as the monastic chronicler Gervase tells us, 'an escaping spark caused a great conflagration and the roof came crashing down'. The question of whether to repair the old or to build a new cathedral occupied the councils of the monks. They had the great good fortune to appoint as architect the most revolutionary figure in the history of medieval cathedral-building in England, William of Sens. To this remarkable Frenchman they entrusted the task and to him we owe the choir of the present cathedral. Unfortunately he was dreadfully injured in a fall from the scaffolding, but by the time he was taken home to France to die the choir had reached as far as the transepts, and a second architect – another William, this time William the Englishman – was appointed. He continued building eastwards: the transepts, the Trinity Chapel, the corona (Canterbury's most sparkling and unique feature) and the extension to the crypt. All had to be not only to the glory of God but to commemorate the man now universally regarded as one of the Church's greatest saints, Thomas à Becket. Even before the two Williams had completed their building, churches had been dedicated to the martyr's honour throughout Europe and pilgrims were already flocking to Canterbury to venerate the saint and to visit the site of his murder and the place of his burial. After Henry II came Louis VII of France, the first King of France ever to visit England. He came to pray for his sick son and when he left Becket's tomb he placed upon it his most precious jewel. Known as the Regale of France, it was to remain the richest treasure of the shrine until it was seized as plunder and turned into a ring for Henry VIII nearly four hundred years later.

In 1220, six years after the death of William the Englishman, St Thomas's body was translated to its shrine at the east end of the choir. Two years before, Archbishop Langton (one of the heroes of the Magna Carta and the man who divided the Bible into chapters) had proclaimed the date of the translation. The ceremony must have been glitter-ing and imposing. Not only Canterbury but the surrounding countryside was full

> Of bishops and abbots, priors and parsons,
> Of Earls and of barons, and many knights thereto;
> Of serjeants and of squires, and of husbandmen enow.
> And of simple men eke out of the land.

Henry III headed the procession, which included not only the Archbishop but the Papal Nuncio and the Primate of France. Until 1536 this day, 7 July, was annually celebrated as the Festival of Translation of the Blessed St Thomas.

The lierne vaulting with its magnificent collection of roof bosses, in the north walk of the cloister.

Though the shrine was plundered and desecrated at the time of the dissolution of the monasteries, there is a representation of it in one of the windows of the cathedral and we have numerous accounts of its sumptuous splendour. Supported on marble arches, the shrine itself was concealed under a wooden covering. When the pilgrims were duly

The Norman crypt, the finest in England,
looking east.

assembled on their knees, this cover was suddenly raised to reveal an extraordinary creation of gold and precious stones, foremost among which was King Louis's great jewel. Canterbury became, after Jerusalem and Rome, perhaps the chief place of Christian pilgrimage, and the pilgrims brought with them offerings and, by their very presence, a prosperity which enabled further money to be lavished upon the cathedral. Every English king came to Canterbury – even, at the beginning of his reign, Henry VIII – and many of these royal visitors gave handsomely. In 1299 Edward I gave the crown of Scotland to adorn Thomas's shrine. One of Canterbury's most illustrious visitors was Edward the Black Prince, son of Edward III. He was buried here, and with the shrine of Becket gone his tomb is now generally regarded as Canterbury's greatest glory.

Building continued throughout the fourteenth century. The choir screen and part of the chapter-house were built in the first twenty years, to be followed by the Black Prince's chantry. The nave and south transept are the work of Henry Yevele, foremost of medieval architects, who was also responsible for part of the cloisters. Early in the fifteenth century the chapter-house was completed and the cathedral given its south-west tower and Henry IV's chapel.

The second half of the fifteenth century saw the completion of the cathedral with the north transept and Lady Chapel, and, above all, the immaculately beautiful central tower known ever since as Bell Harry, with its exquisitely lovely vaulting. Thus by the beginning of the fifteenth century the cathedral was as we know it, though the north-west tower was reconstructed, exactly to match the south-west tower, between 1834 and 1841.

Canterbury suffered two great spates of destruction. The first was when Henry VIII reviled St Thomas, proclaimed him a traitor and had his shrine plundered. The second came a century later when the fanaticism of the Puritans was expressed in an excess of iconoclastic zeal, partly because of the extreme unpopularity with the Puritans of Archbishop Laud, who was beheaded for his loyalty to Charles I. There are horrifying accounts of this later destruction. In 1642 Cromwellian troopers cut the altar rail to pieces and then 'threw the altar over and over down the three altar steps and left it lying with the heels upwards'. Later the newly erected font was pulled down, the inscriptions, figures and coats of arms, graven upon brass, were torn from the ancient monuments. 'Whatever there was of beauty or decency in the holy place was despoiled.' Windows were smashed and lead stripped from the roof, water tanks and pipes. The choir was 'stripped and robbed of her fair and goodly hangings'. Organ, communion table, and much of the rest of the furniture were destroyed. By the time of the restoration of Charles II in 1660 'so little had the fury of the late reformers left remaining of it besides the bare walls and roofs, and these partly through neglect, and partly by the daily assaults and batteries of the disaffected, so shattered, ruinated and defaced as it was not more unserviceable in the way of a cathedral than justly scandalous to all who delight to serve God in the beauty of holiness.'

Notwithstanding this orgy of destruction, Canterbury's central position as the first cathedral of the Church of England ensured that restoration was undertaken and some of the seventeenth-century work, especially the canons' stalls, was of superb quality.

In spite of all this havoc visitors today can still follow the processional route the pilgrims trod. The most remarkable feature of the cathedral, and that which impresses itself immediately on any visitor, is the fact that it is on a series of levels. The choir is above the nave, the presbytery and altar are above the rest of the choir, the Trinity Chapel and corona higher still. So we can see how the pilgrims ascended to the shrine, and although the shrine is not there now we can see the marvellous pavement, brought back by the Crusaders, which surrounded it. The journey takes us through the forest of columns which is the nave, a masterpiece of the early Perpendicular style, and through the superbly carved stone pulpitum erected by Prior Chillenden at the beginning of the fifteenth century.

The choir of the two Williams, William of Sens and William the Englishman, is Canterbury's greatest architectural feature, but there are others which may be even more evocative, such as the hollows in the steps to the Trinity Chapel worn by the feet of generations of pilgrims who came to venerate St Thomas between 1220 and 1538. A remarkable quantity of great glass survives, the best thirteenth-century painted glass in England. There are well-preserved wall paintings too, dating from the twelfth century, in St Gabriel's and St Anselm's chapels, the subject of scholarly recent restoration.

The Black Prince's tomb is not the only one of great magnificence and importance. There is a fine effigy of Henry IV, the only king to be buried at Canterbury, and the wonderful alabaster tomb of Lady Margaret Holland flanked by her two husbands, John Beaufort, Earl of Somerset, and Thomas Plantagenet, Duke of Clarence. The most sumptuous episcopal tomb is that of Henry Chicheley, archbishop from 1414 to 1443, and there is a fine Elizabethan monument to Nicholas Wootton who was dean here, but who declined the offer of the archbishopric.

As with so many of our cathedrals the visitor will miss much if he does not look up, especially to the grace and beauty of the fan vault in the lantern of the Bell Harry Tower and to the remarkable series of heraldic roof bosses in Canterbury's lovely cloisters, which are themselves part of fascinating and extensive monastic precincts, the most interesting feature of which is the monks' water tower.

In the twentieth century the cathedral has been lovingly cared for and restored but more has been done than merely conserve the glories of the past. What was formerly known as the Corona Chapel has been rededicated to the Saints and Martyrs of the twentieth century, and some very fine twentieth-century stained glass has been installed in the south-east transept – four jewel-like windows by Erwin Bossanyi.

For all its individual beauties, and in spite of the fact that some of the things here are the very best of their kind, it is Canterbury's historical associations which make it the most special of English cathedrals. It is a place where almost every visitor becomes a pilgrim.

The effigy of the Black Prince is Canterbury's most famous royal monument and, since the destruction of Becket's shrine, its most notable tomb.

CARLISLE

The Cathedral of the Holy and Undivided Trinity

As a guide book to Carlisle Cathedral published at the turn of the century rather quaintly puts it, 'Carlisle is not a large or notable Cathedral, but its delightful Early English Choir with its magnificent East Window will ever redeem it from being insignificant or uninteresting.' There are indeed things to admire in Carlisle, not least the very obvious love and care that has been lavished upon the building over the last century, but if you are not to be disappointed it is as well to dispell all thoughts of, and comparisons with, the great cathedrals of England before going to Carlisle. Forget grandeur, do not expect to be awed, and you will enjoy your visit to this, perhaps the least known of all English cathedrals.

Thanks to the destruction and havoc wrought during the Civil War, Carlisle is (after Oxford) the second smallest of English cathedrals, but it is an ancient foundation. It has a history as interesting as, and more troubled than, almost any other church still in use – and it is the only English cathedral which has with the fortunes of war found itself in different countries. For Carlisle was fought over by English and Scots for nearly five hundred years, and later, during the 1745 Jacobite Rebellion, it was once more a disputed town.

An exterior view.

This was a wild and desolate land when St Cuthbert first came here in 685, two years before his death on the Holy Island of Lindisfarne, and although the remains of a Saxon Cross give evidence of Christian worship here in the dark days before the city was laid waste by the Danes in 875, Carlisle's strategic position was not conducive to the establishment of any centre for the contemplative life.

William Rufus, the Conqueror's son, took the city in 1092 and set about establishing English rule. A religious community was seen as a necessary part of that establishment but it was not until 1122 that Henry I was responsible for bringing the Augustinian Canons to take charge of this border priory.

The south aisle of the original seven-bay Norman nave.

The choir screen, dating from the late fifteenth century and bearing the arms of Bishop Percy and the Neville family.

Even then the Black Canons, as they were called from the colour of their habits, still owed allegiance to the Bishop of Glasgow and it was to make the new border city entirely English that in 1133 Henry created the see of Carlisle and made his father confessor Adelulf, prior of the abbey, its first bishop. The only Augustinian priory to become an English cathedral, Carlisle included in its diocese most of the present county of Cumbria.

Its early history was a turbulent one. The area was poor, border troubles frequent and there were long periods when the see was vacant. In 1218 Carlisle was even briefly in Scottish hands again. In 1292 a fire damaged the Norman cathedral. In 1297 Robert Bruce swore allegiance to Edward I, but that did not bring peace, and in 1304 Edward granted special compensations to the prior and his canons for the many houses and churches which had been burned

by the Scots. In 1307 Bruce was excommunicated by the Papal Legate, in the presence of Edward, for repudiating the oath which he had taken on the sword of St Thomas of Canterbury.

By this time the cathedral consisted of its original Norman nave, with seven bays, and a choir which had twice been rebuilt, once at the beginning of the thirteenth century and again after the fire of 1292. This was, and remains, the glory of the church. During the fifteenth century, times being less troubled, much effort and skill were spent on adorning and beautifying this choir. Fine choir stalls were provided, noted today for their exuberant and entertaining misericords. We can still enjoy the lively imagination of the carvers who lavished

One of the exuberant and ingenious misericords; it shows a kilted man being swallowed by a dragon.

their skill on creating dragons, a fox killing a goose, a mermaid with a looking-glass, and other medieval scenes and fancies. During the same century the choir screen was erected, with the armorial bearings of William Percy, Bishop of Carlisle from 1452 to 1462, to the north, and those of the great Neville family to the south. Stained glass was installed and painters adorned walls and ceilings with signs and symbols, and with colourfully graphic accounts of the lives of St Augustine, St Cuthbert and St Anthony. This, of course, was the time when an illiterate population absorbed the stories of the Old and New Testaments and of the great Christian saints from the representations they saw in churches.

There was no further major building and this was the cathedral the Augustinians had to surrender to Henry VIII when he dissolved the monasteries. Immediately, however, he refounded the see and the last prior became the first dean, and the cathedral was given a new dedication, to the Holy and Undivided Trinity. The nave, however, remained St Mary's and was given to the town as its parish church. The Dean, Lancelot Salkeld, was deprived of his office by Edward VI and restored to it by the

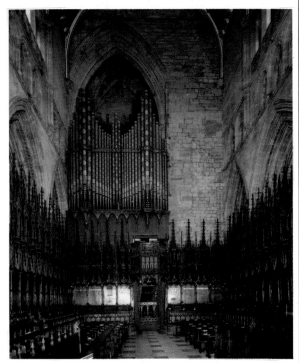

Carlisle's glorious chancel.

Catholic Mary Tudor, only to be deprived again by Elizabeth. Carlisle's leading clerics were much in the national eye at this time, for the bishop at Elizabeth's succession, Owen Oglethorpe, was the only bishop then in office who was prepared to crown the new queen. He did so, but the full Catholic ritual he insisted upon so angered her that he lost her favour and within a year he was deposed. The silver wand with which Carlisle's verger led him at the coronation service in the abbey is still used in the cathedral.

The early seventeenth century was a time of neglect. There are accounts of the cathedral's being sorely in need of repair by the time of the great siege of Carlisle in 1644. This was the most disastrously destructive chapter in any English cathedral's history. By the end of it only two bays of the Norman cathedral were left. The stones of the others had been carted off to build fortifications. The chapter-house was destroyed, the library was ransacked and the plate melted down for coinage.

At the time of the Restoration the building was described as being 'black but comely, still bearing the remaining signs of former burning'. After 1660, however, repairs were effected, a new library was built and the dean, Thomas Smith, later to become bishop, was zealous in his efforts to build and restore.

In the eighteenth century there were further problems. Jacobite prisoners were housed in the cathedral during the '45 Rebellion. There were attempts at restoration but, as one authority has it, 'they for the most part consisted of hiding the beautiful choir roof with a stucco groined ceiling, and plentifully whitewashing the building'. Towards the end of the eighteenth century, however, Carlisle was becoming something of a centre of learning. Perhaps the most influential of all those associated with it (and they included the Cambridge divines Edmund Law, bishop from 1769 to 1787, and Willam Paley, who was archdeacon) was Isaac Milner who was dean from 1792 to 1820. His was one of the most active and brilliant minds of the late eighteenth century. He was a leading evangelical and the man responsible for William Wilberforce's conversion.

Carlisle was fortunate throughout the nineteenth century. Bishop Tate, later to be Archbishop of Canterbury, brought in Ewan Christian to conduct the extensive restoration of the cathedral. It is to him that we mainly owe the building as it is today.

The painted wooden ceiling of the chancel – an attractive
nineteenth-century re-creation.

He was followed by a veritable procession of notable ecclesiastical architects, including Street and Blomfield, and, in more recent years, Charles Nicholson and Steven Dykes-Bower. The result is a building that is more like a very fine and carefully tended parish church than a noble cathedral but, considering the destruction and desecration of the Civil War, it is really a triumph of love and ingenuity over adversity that has preserved the best of the old within a carefully guarded living church.

The first thing that the visitor notices today is that the Norman arches which remain are misshapen. This is a result of droughts in the middle of the thirteenth century which so disturbed the water table that the ground settled unevenly. But if the Norman work is strangely preserved, the Early English chancel is a joy, with its sculpted capitals representing the months of the year, its misericords, wall paintings which have been carefully restored, and a painted wooden ceiling, attractively re-created in the nineteenth century.

There is a fine east window with delicate and elaborate tracery, and there are more recent treasures too, the most notable of which is the Brougham Triptych, a superb Flemish altarpiece brought here as recently as 1979.

CHICHESTER

The Cathedral of the Holy Trinity

Chichester's spire is the only one of England's cathedral towers visible from the sea. It is a landmark for mariners and the story of the spire, its rise and fall and rise again, dominates the history of the cathedral as the spire itself dominates the skyline. There is another notable tower here too, for Chichester is the only cathedral which still has its original detached bell tower. (Such towers were often built to house cathedral bells and so relieve the strain on the main fabric.)

Chichester was one of the first of the Norman sees. As we have seen before, it was William the Conqueror's policy to site his cathedrals in important towns and so in 1075 the ancient diocese of Selsey, founded by Wilfrid in 709, became the diocese of Chichester.

It was the second archbishop, Ralph de Luffa (1091–1123), who was the first great builder. There was a severe fire in 1114 but much of the cathedral

Chichester's spire, for long a landmark for sailors.
It is Scott's Victorian replacement of the
one which collapsed in 1861.

we know today dates from his time – nave, transepts, choir, and the three chapels to the east. In 1187, while Seffrid II was bishop (1180–1204), another fire swept the building, destroying the roof and much of the east end. As a result a stone vault was erected above the new clerestory and it is to this rebuilding that we owe the splendid arches and the Purbeck marble shafts which are such a distinguishing feature of the nave. Seffrid's major achievement was the superb retrochoir, perhaps the finest example of the so-called Transitional style which bridged Norman and Gothic. In the thirteenth century more chapels were added in the nave, and the cathedral acquired a shrine, the tomb of the saintly Richard of Wych, bishop from 1245 to 1253. Originally at odds with the king, Henry III, he so impressed his flock by the pastoral care with which he looked after them when exiled from his own cathedral, and proved such a model bishop when he was allowed to come to Chichester, that he was canonized within nine years of his death. In 1276 his body was transferred from its first resting-place by a pillar near the Chapel of St Thomas to a new shrine behind the high altar, dedicated in the presence of Edward and his queen and the Archbishop of Canterbury. Some of the arrangements sound rather macabre. His head was chopped off and placed in a recess in the Chapel of St Mary Magdalene, and the Archbishop of Canterbury took an arm home with him (exchanged two hundred years later when a relic of St Wilfrid was sent from Canterbury to Chichester). Henceforth pilgrims came in great numbers to the shrine, and in recent years the custom has been revived by modern pilgrims eager to express their devotion and their belief in the continuing importance of piety and pastoral care.

In the fourteenth century the Lady Chapel was extended, the great window in the south transept put in, and the choir stalls erected. Though they were restored in the nineteenth century after the collapse of the spire, the canopies of these stalls are original and they have a splendid series of misericords. Like those in many of England's cathedrals the carvings on these are exuberant and secular – perhaps, it has been suggested, because

The only surviving detached bell tower in any English cathedral. It stands to the north of the west front and dates from the mid-fifteenth century.

medieval carvers would not have people, even the clergy, sitting on saints and angels.

The fifteenth century saw the cathedral completed. The cloisters were built around 1400, about the same time as the great window in the north transept was inserted. During the first half of the century the bell tower and the spire were built. Later still the great stone pulpitum across the nave was added. Known as the Arundel Screen (after Bishop John Arundel, 1459–78), it was taken away by the Victorians just before the collapse of the spire and restored a hundred years later, in 1960, as a memorial to the greatest of Chichester's twentieth-century bishops, the famous Bishop Bell.

The screen behind the high altar was installed by the last of the great pre-Reformation bishops, Robert Sherbourne. He was an important councillor of state, Chancellor to Henry VII and one of the King's ambassadors. His effigy is the finest in the cathedral. It is also one of the earliest true likenesses. Before the sixteenth century effigies on tombs normally bore absolutely no resemblance to the departed. Those erecting them would merely purchase an appropriate figure from the sculptor. It was rather like buying a gravestone from a monumental mason's catalogue today. Bishop Sherbourne died in 1536 and within a few years the

reformers had sought to purge this cathedral, as they purged most others, of anything that smacked of idolatry. The shrine of St Richard was destroyed and his bones scattered. Commissioners from the King came with orders to destroy all monuments that had received 'the honour due to God alone'. It was a convenient way of combining apparent purity with real cupidity, for from here, as elsewhere, precious stones and metals from the shrine swelled the royal coffers.

During the Civil War and the Commonwealth a new generation of zealots wrought further havoc and because of these successive visitations of

One of a pair of magnificent Romanesque relief sculptures, Chichester's greatest glory. This is a detail from the Raising of Lazarus.

vandals Chichester has no medieval glass. Efforts were made to restore the cathedral after Charles II returned to the throne, and towards the end of the seventeenth century Christopher Wren was employed in rebuilding the spire. He was also commissioned to rebuild the west end but those plans were never carried out.

The familiar story of eighteenth-century indolence succeeded by nineteenth-century restoration

The retrochoir, the finest feature of Chichester, built after the fire in 1186 in the Transitional style, between Norman and Gothic.

was repeated here but Chichester's restoration was more dramatic than most. A cathedral which had experienced the collapse of a tower, severe fires in the Middle Ages and pillaging in the seventeenth century suffered its most dramatic disaster in 1861. During January of that year there was mounting concern at cracks that had appeared in the tower and the surrounding fabric. When the walls of the north-west and then of the south-west pier began to bulge, desperate attempts were made to shore them up with timber. Throughout January and early February the work went on, but on 20 February mortar began to crumble and flakes of stone began to fall. The work of rescue continued until 3.30 on the morning of 21 February. Before dawn seventy men struggled in wild winds to bring more timber to shore up the walls, but to no avail. Around midday the battle was given up and at 1.30 p.m. the tower and spire collapsed, telescoping into the central crossing.

George Gilbert Scott was commissioned to re-build the spire, a task that he accomplished with enormous success, for this is one of the most graceful and majestic of English spires. Major restoration continued and the north-west tower was not finally rebuilt until 1901 by John Lough-borough Pearson, the architect of Truro.

Though Chichester's nave is fine, its retrochoir magnificent, and its wooden vaulted cloisters splendidly proportioned, its greatest treasures are two extraordinary Romanesque carvings on the south wall. Where they came from we are not sure but they are among the greatest of all English cathedral treasures. These early twelfth-century works depict the Raising of Lazarus and Christ being greeted at Bethany by Mary and Martha. Somehow the artists have imbued them both with the intensity of a deep but simple faith, strongly held.

In the Lady Chapel there are still the remains of a very fine roof painting. The railings around the chapel are made up from iron grilles that came from the shrine of St Richard. Among Chichester's other prized possessions is the thirteenth-century effigy of Maud, Countess of Arundel. That of Richard Fitzallen, Earl of Arundel, at the end of the four-teenth century, was over-sentimentally restored in the nineteenth century when his hand was placed in that of his countess.

Chichester has more recent treasures too. There are some particularly fine memorials by Flaxman and, largely owing to the determination of Dean Hussey in the 1960s to make the church again a patron of the arts, there are remarkable twentieth-century things. It is easy to dismiss some of them as being incongruous but those who do so forget what Chichester – and almost every other cathedral – tells us, that successive generations, in their different ways and styles, have sought to glorify God through carved and painted ornament. Perhaps some of the more recent additions to Chichester will be as little regarded in a hundred years' time as we regard most of the rather disappointing Victorian glass that is here. But if the Victorians had not had the audacity to make stained glass England's churches and cathedrals would be far poorer.

Here at Chichester some of the modern furnishings are so daringly contemporary that they run the risk of clashing with hallowed stones and wood. The most stunning and startling of them is John Piper's tapestry which hangs beneath the medieval canopies of the Sherbourne screen: seven strips of symbolic colour, woven near Aubusson and installed here in 1966. Then there is the Chagall window, put in in 1978, a symphony in red designed to illustrate Psalm 150, 'O Praise God in his holiness ... Let everything that hath breath praise the Lord'.

In contrast to these is the simple altar by Robert Putter in the Chapel of St Mary Magdalene, with Graham Sutherland's small masterpiece, *Noli Me*

The monument to Robert Sherbourne on the south wall. It is the finest effigy in the cathedral and one of the first true likenesses (1536).

The nave showing the Norman arches with their Purbeck marble shafts and the triforium with clerestory above.

Tangere, above. In the Chapel of St Clement is another altar frontal, the Icon of Divine Light, by Cecil Collins.

It took courage to bring these representations of the twentieth century into this ancient cathedral, but it is a courage that merely continues and echoes that inspiration and ingenuity responsible for Bishop Arundel's screen, the Chichester misericords and those acts of Norman homage, the cathedral's most lasting treasures.

DURHAM

The Cathedral Church of Christ and Blessed Mary the Virgin

Perched on the wooded cliffs above the river Wear, Durham has the most awe-inspiring setting of any building in Britain. It is fitting that it should, for this is acknowledged to be the finest of England's Norman churches, and indeed the greatest Romanesque church in Europe. I first saw it in the fading light of a dull winter's day from the window of a railway carriage, and no building has ever made such an impact on me. Massive, magisterial, commanding the town and dominating the skyline, it was all and more than I had been told. Every visit and every subsequent glimpse from road or train can only serve to reinforce that impression. Every time I see the cathedral I think of Scott's lines:

> Grey towers of Durham, yet well I love thy mixed
> and massive piles,
> Half church of God, half castle 'gainst the Scot.

Built as a shrine for one of the most venerated of English saints, and until 1836 the seat of a prince bishop who presided with almost royal powers over the county palatine of Durham, the cathedral is unlike any other in England both in the majesty of its homogeneous architecture and in the fascination of its history.

When Cuthbert, Prior of Lindisfarne, died on Holy Island in 687, he gave his monks a sacred charge. If they ever had to leave that holy place they were to take his bones with them. Harried by invaders from the north, the successors of those monks were forced to abandon Lindisfarne two centuries later, but they remembered the saint's injunction and they bore his coffin away with them. We are told that for seven years they wandered the wastelands, moors and forests of Northumbria before coming to rest at Chester-le-Street. But even there they were not safe from marauding invaders and in 999, having been on their travels again, the community at last found a home on the cliffs above the Wear at Durham. The task of building a church for the religious offices and a shrine for the saint's bones began. Durham is the only cathedral to have been built as a shrine – but of that first church there is no trace. The second still remains. Between 1093 and 1133, only forty years, the great cathedral was built and the bones of Cuthbert and of the Vener-

Looking proud over the Wear – 'half church of God, half castle 'gainst the Scot'.

able Bede, stolen and brought here from Jarrow by a monk, were given a permanent resting place.

The foundation stone was laid by Bishop de St Carileph, second Bishop of Durham, watched by Malcolm, King of the Scots, the man who slew Macbeth. Only two men, William and his successor Ranulph Flambard, together with the monks and the Benedictine community they ruled, can claim credit for the church. The speed with which they worked was remarkable, the more so because it was the first church in north-west Europe planned from the beginning to be covered throughout with stone vaulting. As an abbey church and cathedral it was unique, too, in that the bishop, not the abbot, ruled and had first place within the church as well as in the diocese.

The high altar and magnificent Neville screen,
carved in Caen stone c. 1380.

This was a great and rich community. The shrine of Cuthbert was a sacred and venerated, and a much visited, place. Not unnaturally the mighty cathedral was further embellished and adorned, though we may give praise that there was never any attempt to demolish what the great Norman bishops had achieved or fundamentally to change it. Immediately after the completion of the main church a chapter-house was added, and then, at the end of the twelfth century, the beautiful Galilee Chapel with its slender piers (subsequently strengthened) and remarkable chevron decoration. Early in the thirteenth century the west towers were completed and between 1242 and 1280 the Chapel of the Nine Altars was built, a miracle of grace which blends remarkably happily with the earlier Norman round arches. It was so called because of the need for numerous altars at which to celebrate the Mass. The great window in the north wall is the finest piece of Gothic design at Durham.

In the middle of the fourteenth century the great west window was added and a few years later John, Lord Neville, gave the imposing reredos known as the Neville screen, which still stands behind the high altar. Made in Caen stone and carved in London (possibly by Henry Yevele, master architect of Westminster Hall and much of the Abbey), it was brought in pieces by sea to Newcastle and then assembled by local masons. It suffered much at the hands of the iconoclasts after the Reformation, but it is still a noble work.

As with so many of our cathedrals, the centre tower was subject to the hazards of lightning. Its final rebuilding towards the end of the fifteenth

*The view east down the nave, looking towards the choir
with its fine Charles II stalls.*

The Galilee Chapel, built as a Lady Chapel and notable for its graceful pillars and chevron decoration.

century was the last pre-Reformation work done at Durham. The monks were obliged to surrender the monastery to the King in 1540. The familiar story of statue breaking was repeated, though here it carried on much longer, for it was a particularly Puritan dean in the reign of Elizabeth who was responsible for much of the destruction in Durham, acting from that pious bigotry which did so much to rob England of her medieval treasures.

Cuthbert's body – still, we are told, in a perfect state of preservation – was buried under a plain slab and his shrine was plundered. There he still rests, together with the head of Oswald, King of Northumbria, who founded the see of Lindisfarne in 635.

In 1650, after the battle of Dunbar, Cromwell locked four thousand prisoners in the cathedral and they used the choir stalls as firewood. Fortunately Durham had a great bishop at that time, John Cosin,

who returned to his post after the restoration of Charles II. To Bishop Cosin we owe the fine choir stalls we see today, and the magnificent carved canopy over the font. In spite of his careful and loving stewardship, however, Durham did not escape the effects of that century of slumber which is the history of the Church of England in the eighteenth century, until in 1777 interest in the fabric was stirred when the architect reported that the building was in a dangerously dilapidated state. James Wyatt was brought in to supervise the restoration, but thankfully his attempts at major changes were frustrated. One look at Hereford makes us realize what a narrow escape Durham had.

The restorations of the nineteenth century in which Sir George Gilbert Scott, that most energetic of restorers, had a hand, were reasonably restrained and some of the less attractive alterations, such as the removal of the great clock from the south transept, have since been put right, though no one has had the courage to tackle Scott's pulpit and screen.

In recent years a beautiful tester has been hung over the tomb of St Cuthbert. Designed by Sir Ninian Comper, it shows Christ in Majesty surrounded by the symbols of the Evangelists. The wooden screen which separates the shrine from the Nine Altars transept, removed a century ago, was restored in 1936. Most of the efforts of the twentieth century have been directed towards preserving what the Normans and their immediate descendants gave us, a building of incomparable unity and majesty.

Durham has few major memorials, mainly because it was considered improper to bury anyone within a building which was erected as the shrine of a great saint, and for many years no one was buried here. Among its tombs are those of the early bishops in the chapter-house and, in the Chapel of the Nine Altars, of recent deans and prelates, also a memorial to Bishop Mildert, the last of the prince bishops. The greatest memorial, however, is that to Bishop Hatfield (1318–33), an altar tomb on which is placed the bishop's throne, said to be the loftiest bishop's throne in the Christian Church.

There are many things here worthy of note. There is the sanctuary knocker on the north door – a bronze replica of the original twelfth-century knocker now in the treasury. Any fugitive seizing

Durham's unique twelfth-century sanctuary knocker. The original is now in the treasury and a reproduction on the north door.

this could claim the right of sanctuary. There are fine misericords in the choir stalls, and the simple but moving inscription on the miners' memorial which remembers those who have given their lives in the pits of County Durham, and those who still risk them there. There is Cuthbert's coffin, and, in the treasury, the Anglo-Saxon stole it once contained. The Monks' Door into the west cloister has ironwork that has been there since the cathedral was first consecrated 850 years ago. And there is the monks' dormitory, still with its original roof timbers, and now an important museum.

The greatest treasure of Durham is the building itself, the noblest of Norman churches, with a nave so impressive, yet simple, that its massive dignity would be overwhelming were its proportions not so completely perfect as to be uplifting.

The majesty of the finest Romanesque interior in Europe.

ELY

The Cathedral of the Holy Trinity

A good imagination is an essential qualification for the full enjoyment of most noble buildings, and in the case of Ely Cathedral this is particularly so. It can still bring a thrill to the dullest motorist as he drives along the flat Fenland roads, but to envisage Ely's challenging beauty to the full we have to imagine it rising above the waters of the undrained Fen. No wonder it was often likened to a great ship. To get a true idea of the power of faith in the Middle Ages we need only think of this great church, the centre of an isolated religious community, set in the bleak marshes of East Anglia. With no town to serve, the monks who spent their days there did indeed do all 'to the Glory of God'.

It was originally a Saxon nunnery, founded in 673 by St Etheldreda, Queen of Northumbria, who came here and established a religious community in which the two succeeding abbesses were also widowed Saxon queens. Of this time there is only one reminder in the cathedral, the Ovin Stone, the base of a Saxon cross rescued by an eighteenth-century antiquary from use as a mounting block in a nearby village, and brought back to the cathedral.

The house of prayer founded by Etheldreda was pillaged by the Danes in 869 but refounded as a Benedictine monastery a century later. Still there were turbulent times ahead. It was the last outpost of the Saxon hero Hereward the Wake. His campaigning caused such privations that the secret of his stronghold was surrendered and in 1081 William I appointed Abbot Symion to take charge. The abbot was a man in whom William placed absolute and justified faith, although he was eighty-six years old. He lived for another twelve years and began the building of a second great abbey church, creating a shrine to Etheldreda to the east of the high altar.

Building continued throughout the twelfth century and was completed around 1189. In 1109 the abbey church became a cathedral when the Pope agreed that the abbot should be bishop of a new

Ely cathedral standing high above the flat lands of the Fens. Before the Fens were drained it rose above the waters, majestic and isolated.

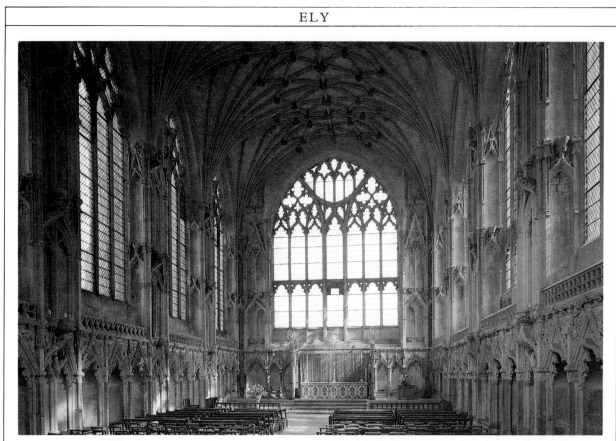

Ely's Lady Chapel, north-east of the north transept, is the largest in England and has the widest of all medieval vaults. Its greatest glory is its Decorated arcades, remarkable for their nodding ogees.

diocese created from part of the enormous diocese of Lincoln. We can enjoy much of this Norman church in a way that we can appreciate few others, for it is the practice at Ely to keep the nave clear of chairs so that the visitor can get some conception of what a great medieval cathedral was really like.

The superb Galilee porch at the west end was added early in the thirteenth century, and later in the same century Bishop Hugh created a magnificent presbytery, consecrated in 1252 in the presence of King Henry III. Fine as this work is, and much as it is rightly admired, Ely's two greatest glories were still to come. They were the conception of one of the most remarkable of that extraordinary group of medieval building clerics who created some of the noblest buildings in the land. Alan of Walsingham, sacrist in the abbey, was in charge of building when in 1322 the Norman central tower collapsed. It was his idea to build in its place Ely's unique feature – the superb octagon. From the eight pillars, the glorious lantern rises up on corner posts, each cut from a massive oak tree. Conceived in a moment of sublime inspiration and executed by engineers and

The famous lantern tower is one of the supreme masterpieces of medieval engineering and architectural genius.

The spectacular vaulted ceiling of Bishop West's chantry

at the end of the south aisle. It was built in 1533.

The view from the choir to the west door, showing the painted ceiling of the Norman nave and the octagon over the crossing.

craftsmen of unsurpassed skill, there is nothing like it in the whole of Europe. It has the power to move (quoting from the famous prayer of Bishop Gunning of Ely, who is buried in the cathedral) 'all sorts and conditions of men'.

It has been rightly said that the octagon would be regarded as a work of engineering genius in any age, but it was not Alan's only majestic addition to Ely. He was also responsible, with one of his monks, John of Wisbech, for Ely's Lady Chapel. Set between the presbytery and the transept, this miracle of the mason's art, with a roof which has the widest stone vault in England, is like one of the greatest of Norfolk churches, light and spacious, and incredibly beautiful.

The fourteenth century saw Ely virtually complete. An octagonal belfry tower was built at the west end at the same time as the north-west transept collapsed and that is whey the cathedral has its distinctive and curious off-centre appearance, disturbing at first sight but regarded by all who come to know the building with particular affection.

Early in the sixteenth century the two fine chantry chapels of Bishop West and Bishop Allcock were added, built of clunch, a peculiarly hard form of local chalk especially amenable to the mason's chisel.

Within a decade other chisels were being used, for the monastery was dissolved in 1539 and in a destructive and zealous frenzy statues in the Lady Chapel and elsewhere were smashed and defaced and the latest and finest shrine to St Etheldreda was destroyed.

Henry VIII refounded the see and Ely remained a cathedral. Oliver Cromwell, satisfied that enough destruction had been wrought, or out of local affection for something with which he was familiar, spared Ely further assaults, although he was so displeased with its liturgy that he had the cathedral closed throughout the period of his rule.

Although worship resumed with the Restoration in 1660 and there was some repair to the west end towards the end of the seventeenth century (reputedly carried out under the supervision of Christopher Wren, a kinsman of the bishop of the day), this was a period of neglect when Ely was known as the 'dead see'. Stories abound of all manner of non-religious activities, including the breeding and shooting of pigeons, being allowed in the nave.

The first serious attempts at restoration, which included the removal of the medieval screen, began in the mid-eighteenth century. This removal gives us a unique and unbroken vista at Ely such as we can enjoy in no other cathedral. Care and concern for the fabric did not really begin, however, until Dr Peacock was appointed dean in 1839, and it was later in the century that most work was done – much of it by Sir George Gilbert Scott. The most remarkable creation of the period was the nave ceiling which was boarded over and then painted, without fee, by a Mr Le Strange of Hunstanton Hall and his friend, Mr Gambier Parry. It has only recently come to be appreciated as one of the outstanding examples of Victorian ecclesiastical art.

Ely has suffered the ravages of time as much as any great cathedral, and almost continuous restoration projects have been needed throughout the second half of this century. Visitors can, however, get some idea both of the problems and of the beauty of the building by climbing up to the fascinating stained glass museum installed above the nave, and when they have studied its glass, looking down, and up, too – to that extraordinary roof.

The sinuous lines of the elaborately carved
choir stalls on the south side
of the chancel.

EXETER

The Cathedral Church of St Peter

When I was asked to write this book there was only one English medieval cathedral I did not already know and that was Exeter. Though the first visit to any great building is always a memorable experience at first glimpse I was disappointed. Here was no elegance to rival Wells, no grandeur to compare with Durham, no majesty to match Lincoln. Even the unique placing of the two towers, north and south, did not quite compensate. And then we went in. There was the loveliest nave in all England: a stately avenue of Gothic columns, beneath an amazingly beautiful ribbed vault.

Its beauty had obstacles to surmount that morning. For a service in the nave the choir occupied stalls of a particularly solid modern ugliness, a scar that few buildings could withstand, and puny and horrid light fittings hung from iron brackets thrust into the walls. In spite of these blemishes, utilitarianism is vanquished and the visitor to Exeter has an overwhelming feeling that this is a cathedral that is really loved. There is a brightness here that does not owe everything to the clerestories above, or to the sunlight without.

The south tower, one of the two Norman towers which stand, most unusually, over the transepts.

Detail from the elaborately carved west front.

This is an ancient place. The Romans were here and there was a monastery built near the centre of their town within three hundred years of their going. From here Boniface went out to convert the Germans and to be martyred in the course of his mission.

The West Country see, founded at Crediton in 909, was transferred to Exeter to be safe behind the city walls in 1049. Edward the Confessor enthroned Leofric as the first bishop here in 1040, to preside over a diocese that covered the whole of modern Devon and Cornwall. Exeter was another of those cathedrals of the Old Foundation which were never part of a monastery and which were run by secular clergy – initially a group of twenty-four canons, assisted by their deputies or vicars, who sang psalms as they went about their ministry.

Of the Norman cathedral that was built here only the two towers remain. The rest of the existing building owes much to the fact that Bishop Walter Bronescombe was in Salisbury in 1258 at the consecration of Salisbury Cathedral. It doubtless inspired him and his successors to build their own miraculously beautiful cathedral in the Early English style. This is, almost in its entirety, a cathedral

*The early fourteenth-century screen or pulpitum
adorned by seventeenth-century paintings and
surmounted by the massive organ.*

choir stalls there are the earliest misericords in England, a set of forty-nine, dating from the second half of the thirteenth century. Just half a century later the great stone pulpitum was built. This superb choir screen of Purbeck marble is adorned by seventeenth-century painted panels depicting scenes from the life of Christ. It is surmounted by a magnificent seventeenth-century organ case which some think mars the view down the nave towards the great east window with its fourteenth-century glass. Among the greatest treasures of Exeter are the recently re-coloured corbels which decorate the nave, and the minstrels' gallery high above them on

*The famous corbel, one of a series,
showing an acrobat performing before
the Virgin Mary.*

of the thirteenth and fourteenth centuries and nothing, save two chantry chapels that were built at the beginning of the sixteenth century, is any later than 1450.

The familiar story of Reformation destruction was repeated here, and even greater damage was inflicted during the period of the Commonwealth, partly perhaps because Exeter was a city closely associated with Charles I, whose queen gave birth to a daughter here in 1644.

After the restoration of Charles II some of the damage was undone, and the inevitable restoration of Victorian times was gentler here than in most of our cathedrals. Then in May 1942, during one of the many air raids over Exeter, the cathedral was hit. We owe much to the total dedication and immaculate craftsmanship of two very remarkable men, Herbert Read of Exeter, an ecclesiastical artist, and George Down, a master mason of genius, who painstakingly restored, to a point where damage can hardly be detected, what had seemed lost for ever.

So it is that today Exeter seems in a far better state of preservation than almost any other ancient English cathedral, its treasures beautifully conserved. Among the most remarkable of these is the fourteenth-century bishop's throne with its towering sixty-foot-high canopy of Devon oak, wonderfully carved. This needed no repair because it was removed from the cathedral during the war. In the

the north side. This gallery, in which the choir still sometimes sings, was erected in the fourteenth century, and around it are a series of musical angels playing bagpipes, recorders, the viol, the harp – a whole orchestra of medieval instruments carved in stone.

Among the chantry chapels is one founded in 1517 by Sir John Speke, the newest and among the finest of Exeter's adornments. There are porcupines carved here – chosen for their spikes, a rebus or heraldic wordplay on Speke's name and a guide to ancient pronunciation, as are the owls commemorating Bishop Oldham (founder of Manchester Grammar School and co-founder of Corpus Christi College, Oxford) in the Chapel of St Saviour and St Boniface in the south aisle.

Among the most splendid tombs and effigies are those of Bishop Walter de Stapledon, High Lord Treasurer to Edward II, who was assassinated because of his association with the King, and the tomb

The tomb of Walter Bronescombe, Bishop of Exeter, who died in 1280. It was principally he who inspired the transformation of the Norman cathedral.

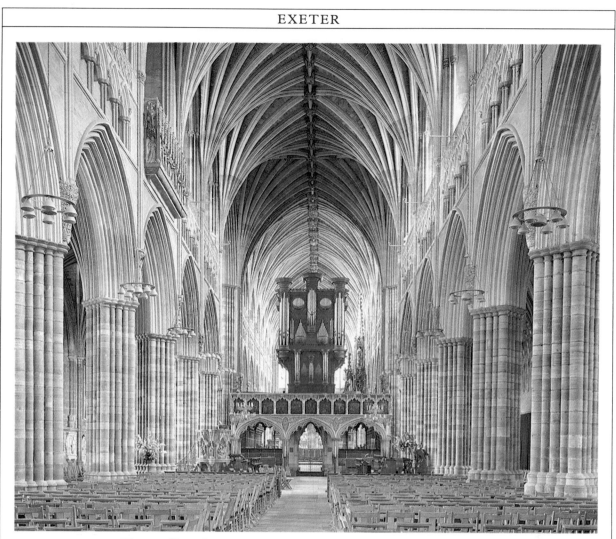

The magnificent Decorated nave with its superb ribbed vault, one of the greatest examples of English Gothic.

of Hugh Courtenay, second Earl of Devon, who has lain here with his wife for six hundred years.

In Exeter, as in so many English cathedrals, it is the little things that are of special delight. There is the famous corbel of an acrobat deploying his talents in honour of the Virgin. There is the sadly mutilated tomb of Sir Richard Stapledon with his pages and horses, and a touching memorial to young Matthew Goodwin who died in 1586 at the age of seventeen and who is written down as a genius 'very worthy and very learned, Master of Music in Canterbury and Exeter Cathedrals'. Just as remarkable in her time was another person commemorated here, Sarah Clark, who we are told had 'a mind which possessed an energy which does not often mark the female character': a phrase which, while doubtless thought unflattering by most people today, never-

theless provokes the thought that an inscription which detailed failings as well as achievements would be a refreshing novelty. It makes one warm to the motto above Bishop Carey's effigy urging that the blood of Christ should cleanse him from his sins. The Carey effigy, incidentally, is a useful reminder of the fact that very often tombs and effigies are different things – in Carey's case, for instance, for he was actually buried in Old St Paul's in London.

Two other things that no visitor should miss are a wood carving of Devon shepherds watching their flocks, the Christmas homage of a local craftsman five hundred years ago, and, in St James's Chapel, George Down's modern corbels of a rugby forward and one of himself. They make the timelessness which is the hallmark of any great place of worship a moving reality.

HEREFORD

Cathedral of Our Lady and St Ethelbert

Herefordshire, one of the loveliest of English counties, is rich in remarkable churches, and those who have fallen under the spell of Abbey Dore or Kilpeck may not be as impressed by the cathedral. It has a splendid aspect when seen across the Wye, its massive central tower dominating the town, and within the cathedral are many fine things, but of all the great English cathedrals none has suffered more at the hands of the restorers and 'improvers'.

Hereford, established in 676, is one of the very oldest English dioceses. Of the first cathedral, dedicated to St Ethelbert, king and martyr, there is no trace. There is, however, much fine Norman work, dating from the end of the eleventh and the first half of the twelfth century. That was an important time in the history of Hereford. Politically the city was much involved in the struggle

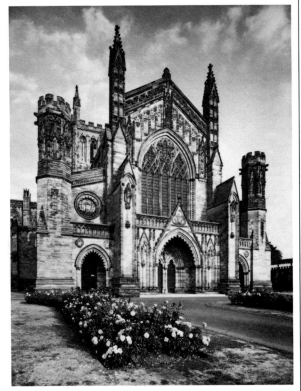

The west front, largely a Victorian recreation, the work of the younger Scott.

between King Stephen and Matilda, and indeed in the sanctuary is an ancient wooden chair on which King Stephen is alleged to have sat when he was enthroned and crowned in the cathedral on the feast of Pentecost in 1138. In the twelfth century too the cathedral was renowned as a seat of learning, and in the wonderfully rich library there are some ninety twelfth-century manuscripts.

In the thirteenth century Hereford had two notable, but very different, bishops. In 1239 Peter Aquablanca came here and began an active but contentious episcopate. He was responsible for the rebuilding of the north transept; he introduced a new distinctive form of liturgy and reorganized the administration of the cathedral in the teeth of fierce opposition. Among the Hereford traditions established at this time was the lighting of two candles before the bishop's throne whenever he occupied it, a custom that is still observed.

In 1275 Thomas Cantilupe came to Hereford as bishop. He was already a considerable figure in the land, having been Chancellor of the University of Oxford and also, briefly, Chancellor of England. His episcopate was a brief one, but before he died in Italy in 1282 he had established a reputation for goodness and piety (in spite of having been involved in a long and bitter wrangle with the Archbishop of Canterbury) which led to his becoming a cult figure. When his bones were returned to Hereford, pilgrims flocked there and reported miracles. His shrine became one of the most visited in the land and in 1320 he was canonized as St Thomas Cantilupe. It was from the offerings of the pilgrims that the great central tower was built about this time. A little later in the fourteenth century Hereford was given a chapter-house, one of the loveliest of all we are told, but it was destroyed in the Civil War. Although Hereford was a secular cathedral, administered by a dean and college of canons, the cloisters were added in the fifteenth century when the two fine chantry chapels of Bishop Stanbury and Bishop Audley were also built. There is fine vaulting in both, and in Bishop Audley's chapel (similar to one that marks his resting place in Salisbury, whence he was translated as bishop in 1503) there is a wonderful painted screen. The medieval cathedral was

The chained library – the most extensive library of its kind in any English cathedral – housed in the upper transept and cloister rooms.

completed at the beginning of the sixteenth century by Bishop Booth, who added the handsome outer north porch and the bishop's cloister.

There was much opposition to the doctrines of the Reformation at Hereford and after a royal visitation the dean and some of the canons were deprived of their livings. But in the reign of Elizabeth Hereford enjoyed a golden age. John Bull, one of the principal musicians of the time, was organist and, as in the twelfth century, the academic distinction of many of the canons made Hereford once again a seat of learning. In the seventeenth century Hereford remained staunch to the King and in 1645, the town having changed hands three times, the Scots were repulsed by the Royalists who used as ammunition bullets made from the melted down lead of the chapter-house roof. Later the Parliamentarians garrisoned the town again, only to find themselves roundly rebuked by Dean Croft from a pulpit that is still in the nave.

In the early eighteenth century Hereford had the misfortune to suffer from an active 'improving'

bishop, Philip Bisse, who installed panelling over Norman pillars in the choir and sanctuary, erected strange pillars and a classical altar-piece, and in the process did much to weaken the structure. But not all activity of this time was destructive, for the early eighteenth century also saw the beginning of the Three Choirs Festival, the annual 'music meeting' which to this day alternates between Hereford, Worcester and Gloucester.

It was on Easter Monday, 1786, that Hereford suffered its most disastrous calamity. The west tower collapsed and in its falling destroyed the west front and much of the nave. James Wyatt was employed as restorer but he wrought further havoc. Sir George Gilbert Scott lambasted Wyatt for replacing the Norman triforium and clerestory with what Scott called a wretched design of his own. Wyatt was responsible too for the rebuilding of the west front of the cathedral and for removing the spire which graced the central tower, an act that most who now regard the tower as the cathedral's most noble adornment would readily forgive.

There was more dissension during the early part of the nineteenth century with clerical feuding which makes Trollope's Barchester clergy seem paragons of conciliatory virtue. But in 1832, with the coming of Dean Mereweather who found the services 'a disgrace, a blot on the Church', a new period in Hereford's history began. Then Lewis Cottingham, together with Scott and his son, supervised further massive restoration which again changed the cathedral. The Scotts undid much of Wyatt's work, and the present Victorian west front is entirely the work

The Early English Lady Chapel with its fine lancet windows.

*The fine painted screen of Bishop Audley's chantry, dating from
the fifteenth century.*

of the son. In the present century further changes have taken place. As recently as 1967 George Gilbert Scott's massive screen, now lamented as a lost masterpiece of Victorian art, was ripped out, for taste changes slowly in the Welsh border country.

This account of periods of rancour and unfortunate restorations should not alarm the intending visitor unduly. Though much has been lost, much remains, and Hereford, one of our smaller and more comfortable cathedrals, still contains original furniture. There is, for instance, the magnificent fourteenth-century bishop's throne, as well as the fine misericords under the choir stalls. There is a splendid series of tombs including particularly fine ones of Bishop Booth, Bishop Stanbury and Peter Aquablanca. There are good secular tombs too, of Joanna de Bohun, Countess of Hereford, and

of Baron Peter De Grandison, the great-nephew of St Thomas Cantilupe. There are also the remains of St Thomas's shrine, although that has been somewhat marred by an extraordinary recent addition which looks for all the world like a floating fluorescent tube.

Hereford's greatest glory is its library of 1,500 chained books now kept, after various vicissitudes, in the upper transept and upper cloister rooms. The chains, however, are as they were when the library was housed in the lovely thirteenth-century Lady Chapel. Among the most precious volumes is a copy of the Four Gospels dating from the eighth century, which was given to the cathedral by Bishop Athelstan who died in 1156. It is a treasure of world importance but is rivalled by Hereford's own picture of the medieval world, the extrordinary Mappa

The Mappa Mundi – the late thirteenth-century map of the world, showing Jerusalem as the centre of the universe – drawn by Prebendary Richard of Haldingham.

Mundi, a great map drawn by Prebendary Richard of Haldingham at the end of the thirteenth century. It shows a flat earth with Jerusalem at the centre and has graphic representations of the Garden of Eden and the Tower of Babel. It would gain from being more impressively displayed, and would then contribute to the overall impression that Hereford is among the best cared for of England's great churches.

LICHFIELD

The Church of St Mary and St Chad

Alone among English cathedrals Lichfield has three graceful spires, known locally as 'The Ladies of the Vale', and they give it the most beautiful silhouette of any cathedral in the country. They make us realize what Wells might have looked like from afar.

To say Lichfield does not live up to the expectations excited by the spires is true but unfair, for no cathedral has suffered more from the blows of war and, because of the nature of the sandstone, from the ravages of time. What we see here is in fact a triumph of Victorian rescue. At Lichfield it was not a case of restorers obliterating, rebuilding or altering, but of restorers truly restoring and seeking to recapture past glory without incongruity.

Such was the havoc caused during the Civil War that it is difficult to know precisely what the cathedral looked like before the famous siege of 1643. Nevertheless, this is still a great and glorious building, a fact which we owe to the genius of the Middle Ages, the determined and courageous ambition of a Restoration bishop, and the loving attentions of those who had charge of Lichfield in the nineteenth century.

St Chad is Lichfield's own saint. One of the greatest missionaries of the early English church, he came here in the seventh century and was bishop of all Mercia from 669 until his death near the city's present Stowe Pool on 2 March 672. The see was administered from Lichfield for another four hundred years, but when the Conqueror decreed that cathedrals should be in major centres of population, the vast diocese was administered first from Chester (after 1075) and then from Coventry (after 1095). Lichfield, however, maintained cathedral status for its church and in 1148 the diocese was acknowledged as having two centres. It remained the diocese of Coventry and Lichfield until 1660, though after the dissolution of the monasteries Lichfield was the sole cathedral. From 1660 it was known as Lichfield and Coventry, the precedence of the two cities being reversed because Charles II rated Lichfield's performance in the Civil War very highly. So it remained until 1836, since when Coventry has no longer featured in the designation.

There are no traces of the earlier Saxon churches of St Chad, nor indeed of the first Norman church, built by Bishop Roger de Clinton, who died whilst on the Second Crusade, in 1148. His church was built around the saint's tomb, however, and the shrine made Lichfield a centre of pilgrimage until the Reformation. It was indeed the popularity of St Chad's shrine which led to the replacing of Bishop Clinton's church by the present cathedral. Between 1195 and 1208 the choir and presbytery, choir aisles and central tower were built. The transepts were added between 1225 and 1240, incorporating the Chapel of St Chad's Head in the south side.

Before the nave was rebuilt, the chapter-house was erected, given priority because of the necessity for Lichfield to maintain its dignity and status during the time the leadership of the diocese was constantly being disputed with Coventry. The idea was that each cathedral in turn should elect the bishop and a seemly chapter-house was therefore necessary. This polygonal building, with its central shaft carried through to the chamber above, has been little altered since. There is a wealth of wonderful carving here of a quality almost comparable with the slightly later work in the chapter-house at Southwell.

Lichfield's three spires are known throughout the Midlands as 'The Ladies of the Vale'.

In the last three decades of the thirteenth century the nave, one of the first burgeonings of the Decorated style, was built, and so was the lower part of the west front. Building continued throughout the fourteenth century. By 1320 the west front with its spires was complete, and so was the central tower, itself to be crowned by a spire towards the end of the century. Between 1320 and 1350 the Lady Chapel and presbytery were finished, and save for the rebuilding of the north-west spire early in the sixteenth century the whole cathedral was completed in 1400. It was, in the opinion of two Irish visitors on their way to the Holy Land, 'of the most gracious and wondrous beauty'.

The first object of wondrous beauty to be lost was the glittering shrine of St Chad, pillaged when Henry VIII ordered that all 'objects of idolatory' should be destroyed. The familiar story of the smashing of stained glass and other treasures was repeated here in the mid-sixteenth century, but Lichfield suffered far greater destruction, more indeed than any other great cathedral, during the Civil War.

Lichfield was very much in the eye of the storm of war, dean and chapter declaring for the King and the townsfolk for Parliament. The close was fortified and on St Chad's Day, 2 March 1643, occurred the most famous event in the history of the cathedral when the leader of the Parliamentary forces, Lord Brooke, was shot dead by a sniper from battlements of the cathedral. The man who fired the shot was one of the sons of Sir Richard Dyott, Commander of the cathedral garrison. He was deaf and dumb and it was reckoned by some Royalists that God had used him as an instrument against the profane forces of Parliament.

Those who loved the cathedral had little cause to rejoice, for when the building fell the Parliamentary forces rampaged through it, desecrating and destroying on all sides. Even worse was to come. Prince Rupert expelled the enemy but before they left they further ravaged the place and then, after the city fell finally and firmly into Parliamentary hands, there followed a period of persistent and wilful destruction. Already the central spire had been destroyed in the siege. During the fourteen desolate years after the Royalist defeat (1646–60) the lead was ripped from the roof and the cathedral itself used as a quarry. By the Restoration of Charles II many thought it beyond repair. There was no glass in the windows, the crashing of the steeple had

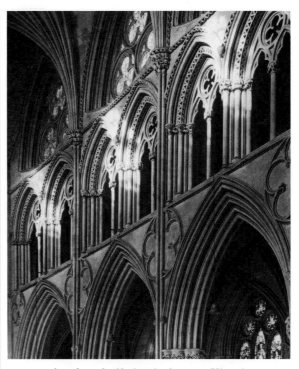

Arcade and triforium in the nave. Victorian restoration has not destroyed the purity of the Gothic form.

smashed the roof in several places, and tombs had been plundered and desecrated.

The clergy who remained thought otherwise. Within a month of Charles II's landing at Dover in May we read that they 'had entered the Chapter House and there said service; and this when the vestry was the only place in the church that had a roof to shelter them'. By July a scheme was afoot for the prebendaries to give one half of their stipends towards the repair of the fabric, 'and by example the gentry would be invited to join with them in some considerable contribution'.

It was a year before Lichfield had a new bishop, for Charles I's bishop had become Archbishop of York immediately after the Restoration. In December 1661, however, John Hacket came from Trinity College, Cambridge, determined that the work that was already begun should be carried to a triumphant conclusion. A redoubtable fund-raiser as well as an enthusiastic lover of the building, he subscribed £1,683 12s to the fund himself, an enormous sum in those days. In eight years the cathedral was transformed from a ruin to a great place of worship again, and at the reconstruction service all the dignitaries

*Sixteenth-century Flemish glass in the Lady Chapel,
brought here in 1795. This detail shows
Mary Magdalene.*

neglect was punctuated by an act of vandalism when the cathedral library was removed in 1757).

As in the neighbouring diocese of Hereford, a realization of the need for repairs came towards the end of the eighteenth century, and the solution was the same: send for James Wyatt. His 'improvements' showed scant regard for the medieval, but at least attention was given to the fabric and one splendid enrichment dates from these times. For it was in 1795 that the cathedral was given some sixteenth-century Flemish glass from the Cistercian abbey of Herckenrode near Liège when that foundation was dissolved by the forces of revolutionary France. The glass was put in the Lady Chapel and remains one of Lichfield's greatest glories.

We are reminded that little changes in the endless debate over what alterations it is right to make to an old building when we read of the Victorians' fierce denunciation of Wyatt's work, with his 'passion for replacing what was old or worn by time with something new'.

The whole of the nineteenth century was a story of change. First Sydney Smirke was appointed architect, as being one of 'sound judgement and experienced in ecclesiastical architecture', and then in 1856 came a major scheme for the restoration of the whole cathedral. George Gilbert Scott was appointed architect and the work was continued by his son John Oldred Scott. Earlier this century it was fashionable to decry the work of Scott (senior) but now the pulpit of brass and iron, with its double staircase, and the chancel screen which he designed are regarded as masterpieces of the Victorian era.

So today we have a great building, conceived in the twelfth and thirteenth centuries, rescued in the seventeenth and then restored almost to the point of re-creation in the nineteenth. Apart from the fact that we can now appreciate that much of what Scott did has an intrinsic beauty of its own the fact is that without his work there would be no cathedral. This was not a case of destroying and starting again. Moreover, the medieval outlines had never been destroyed and much of the grace and beauty of the Early English and Decorated styles – the clustered columns, foliated capitals and richly ornamented triforium – has survived, as has the beautiful tracery of the windows of the Lady Chapel.

Lichfield is not renowned for medieval tombs and effigies but there are fine eighteenth-century busts of Dr Johnson, Lichfield's greatest son, and of

of the diocese, county and city assembled. The bishop 'with a loud voice repeated the first verse of the 144th Psalm, "Blessed be the Lord my strength: who teaches my hands to war, and my fingers to fight".'

It must have been an occasion of remarkable pomp and joy. Much of the great work of the Middle Ages, had, of course, gone beyond recall but there was a new central spire. Lichfield was the most splendid example in the seventeenth century of a whole diocese coming together to rebuild its mother church. Even the King helped by giving '200 fair timber trees out of Needwood Forest', and his brother, the Duke of York, afterwards King James II, gave the money for the tracery of the great west window.

After the triumph of a new awakening came the long sleep which was the history of the Church of England in the eighteenth century. There was no conscious destruction, merely the dilapidation and sad decay which is the inevitable consequence of indolence and neglect (though in this case the

*A detail from the cathedral's greatest treasure
– the eighth-century Gospel of St Chad.*

Sir Francis Chantrey's memorial to the daughters of Canon William Robinson, one of whom perished in a fire.

David Garrick, and a most moving memorial known as 'The Sleeping Children', Sir Francis Chantrey's masterpiece. It represents two daughters of a cathedral prebendary, both of whom died in 1812, one as a result of her dress catching alight at a party. There are later statues of distinction too, including those on the west front, where all but three of the figures are Victorian.

The supreme glory of Lichfield, however, is not carved in stone or wood, but written on parchment. It is the St Chad's Gospel, one of the three or four most beautiful manuscripts in the history of English Christian art. Written and illuminated about 720, it has been here for over a thousand years. Bishops of Lichfield take their oath on it and now it is beautifully displayed in the chapter-house. There could be no more exquisite or evocative link with the saint to whom this cathedral is jointly dedicated.

The nineteenth-century pulpit of brass and iron in the nave, now recognized as one of Scott's masterpieces.

LINCOLN

The Cathedral of the Blessed Virgin Mary

For me Lincoln will always be the supreme English cathedral. The mother church of my native diocese, it was the first cathedral I ever knew and I quickly fell under its spell. I had the privilege, too, of being taken round many times by the late Canon Cook, the greatest authority on the cathedral in living memory. He knew all the secret places, such as where a bored eighteenth-century schoolboy had carved a sailing ship by Bishop Fleming's Chantry. But local pride or early familiarity alone would not have maintained Lincoln's place in my affections. Ruskin reckoned it the finest building in Europe. Alec Clifton Taylor, one of the foremost modern authorities on our cathedrals, counts it 'all things considered, the finest English cathedral'.

Only Durham has a setting that rivals Lincoln's. Crowning the hill, with the ancient town clustered around it, the three towers of this, the most graceful of all medieval buildings, dominate the countryside for miles around, and while other cathedrals have their individual gems of surpassing excellence, none is such a magnificent 'all rounder' as Lincoln. The interior is no disappointment to the new visitor, excited for miles by the distant view of the ark on the waters, as Lincoln was known when the plains around were inclined to flood.

The three towers of Lincoln and its magnificent west front. Originally each tower was surmounted by a spire.

The fine decagonal chapter-house, the stone-vaulted roof fanning out from its graceful central pier.

Lincoln was a great Roman fortress town and when the Romans went it became part of an early Saxon bishopric, almost certainly governed from nearby Stowe, where today one of the greatest of English parish churches stands amidst a cluster of farm buildings. The Danes came and the bishop's seat was moved to Dorchester. The see was re-founded, with Lincoln as its centre, by William the Conqueror and the charter of his first bishop, Remigius, is today one of the cathedral's treasures.

Remigius found himself controlling the largest diocese in England, stretching from the Humber to the Thames, and set about building a cathedral worthy of his charge. Some of his work survives, notably part of the west front, but Lincoln is essentially a product of the twelfth, thirteenth and fourteenth centuries.

From 1135 to 1154, that period known as the nineteen long winters, when the civil war between King Stephen and Empress Matilda raged, Lincoln was fortified by Stephen. Later, in 1185, an earthquake shattered much of the early work. That was the year that Lincoln's greatest bishop, and own saint, came here. Hugh of Avalon was one of the towering figures of the early Middle Ages and at Lincoln he was a great builder as well as a saintly bishop, the first to create a building in which the pointed arch was allowed full play. Under his supervision the earliest and purest form of the Early English style was created. When he died, in 1200, King John and his nobles carried his body to the cathedral door, where it was received by three archbishops and thirteen bishops. The scene is depicted in one of the segments of Lincoln's most famous rose window, known as 'The Dean's Eye'.

As a memorial to the canonized Hugh, and as a fitting setting for his shrine, which became one of the main centres of medieval pilgrimage, almost rivalling the tomb of St Thomas of Canterbury, the great Angel Choir was built, so called from the carvings of angels playing musical instruments above and around the arches. The dedication ceremony in 1280 was attended by Edward I and Queen Eleanor, and for nearly three hundred years pilgrims came with their offerings and their ailments to pray at the glittering shrine. The carving most people readily associate with Lincoln – the tiny mischievous leg-pull by a medieval sculptor which is known as 'the Lincoln imp' – is here in the Angel Choir (and also in a thousand tawdry plaster casts in the gift shops all around).

Lincoln's glorious nave, with its soaring shafts of Purbeck marble, dates from the same century. The central tower we see today was rebuilt after an earlier one had collapsed in 1237. Though the spire

Among the remarkable series of misericords, this one depicts a mounted knight.

The nave looking east through the soaring columns
of Purbeck marble.

*The famous Angel Choir derives its name from the beautifully carved angels in the spandrels,
each playing a different musical instrument.*

that once crowned it has now gone, it remains the most beautifully proportioned of all medieval towers, and the second highest in the country (after the Lincolnshire church tower known as 'the Boston Stump').

Save for three chantry chapels Lincoln was virtually complete as we know it by the early fourteenth century, and only two major alterations took place thereafter. In the seventeenth century Sir Christopher Wren designed the elegant library which occupies one side of the cloisters, and in 1807 the spires on the two west towers were removed.

Lincoln was never a monastic foundation, but as with so many of England's great centres of monastic learning the quality of its spiritual life declined noticeably, and at the visitation of 1500 there were complaints about chaplains playing dice in the chantries, and servants of the dean firing cross-bow bolts at the windows. Sadly, at Lincoln, as elsewhere, the reformers ascribed much of this behaviour to the influence of idolatry, and during the Reformation many of the treasures of the church were smashed and defaced and the shrine of St Hugh was totally destroyed. At the end of the year

1548, we are told, 'there was scarcely a whole figure or tomb remaining'. The work of destruction was completed during the Civil War, when another generation of bigots and zealots gave destructive expression to their prejudices.

Though with the Restoration there was some attempt to restore the cathedral, and a fine new lectern and massive candlesticks were provided, and then Wren's library was built, Lincoln was again neglected during the eighteenth century, as was so common. Its great beauties came to be increasingly appreciated during the nineteenth century, at the end of which Lincoln once more became known for a great saintly bishop, Edward King, whose massive memorial we see in the cathedral today.

If the chief glory of Lincoln is the very fabric of the building itself, nave, choir and Angel Choir, no visitor should fail to allow himself ample time to absorb and appreciate the multitude of other treasures. There is the magnificent screen dividing choir from nave. This masterpiece of the early fourteenth century was restored at the end of the eighteenth by a mason who was anxious to make good some of the damage done by the Puritan soldiers – the only trouble was that he gave bearded mitred heads to all the figures including those of female saints.

Lincoln's choir stalls, with a marvellous series of misericords, are among the finest in the country. There is a wonderful collection of superbly carved corbels and bosses, and much good medieval glass too, in particular two outstanding rose windows known as 'The Dean's Eye' and 'The Bishop's Eye'. The Dean's Eye, over the doors which lead to the old deanery, contains original glass in its original home, and it is here, near the foot, that we can see the burial of St Hugh. The Bishop's Eye, over-looking the old Bishop's Palace, is a kaleidoscope of coloured medieval glass with no pattern at all, gathered up from fragments shattered during the Civil War.

The font, a massive affair of black Tournai marble carved with grotesque animals, was probably made in Flanders in the middle of the twelfth century, about fifty years before the arrival here of one of Lincoln's most renowned treasures, one of the four

Some of the cathedral's finest medieval glass is in the rose window in the north transept – The Dean's Eye.

The famous Lincoln Imp, the mischievous creation of a medieval sculptor.

surviving contemporary copies of Magna Carta, sealed in 1215.

Among those buried in Lincoln is Katherine Swynford, third wife of John of Gaunt and ancestress of the Tudor dynasty. Then there is the fascinating tomb of Bishop Fleming, which is one of the two-tier tombs. We see him above in his bishop's robes and below as a skeleton, a gaunt and startling reminder of how the glories of the world pass away. Another of the cathedral's gems is its chapter-house, perhaps the most beautiful of all the English polygonal chapter-houses, with one soaring central shaft. The first three Edwards all held parliaments here and the bishop's throne was probably theirs.

A visit to the chapter-house is an excuse to take a careful walk around the outside of the cathedral. Many of Lincoln's finest carvings are here, particularly around the west door and the lovely thirteenth-century Judgement Porch and, as Canon Cook used to say, 'the full glory of the east end of Lincoln's cathedral can only fitly be grasped by standing on the green outside the chapter-house', near to the last of Lincoln's great memorials, the statue of Lincolnshire's poet, Alfred Tennyson.

NORWICH

The Cathedral Church of the Holy and Undivided Trinity

*The gracious and elegant
fifteenth-century spire of Norwich
Cathedral.*

Houses and gardens cluster round the cathedral at Norwich creating a wonderful feeling of domestic tranquillity. It is as if the graceful soaring spire is holding court as it rises above the city it has surveyed for five hundred years. Then Norwich was the second city in the kingdom: today it is the least spoilt, and possibly the most lovingly preserved, of England's major county towns. They do not let cars into the close so it is still a real sanctuary.

It was because Norwich was the main town of the area that the East Anglian see, first founded at Dunwich by St Felix in 630 and later divided and based on North Elmham, was moved here from its third centre at Thetford in 1095. There is a unique reminder of those earlier cathedrals in Norwich today: the cathedral houses the only ancient bishop's throne in the country, a chair which includes fragments of the seat on which the Saxon bishops sat. It was brought here by Herbert de

Losinga who laid the foundation stone of his new great cathedral and abbey church in 1096 as an act of penitence for the sin of simony, the purchase of preferment: he had bought the bishopric from William Rufus.

Because Norwich stands on the site of no earlier cathedral it has the most easily traced and perfectly preserved Norman ground-plan of any of the great post-Conquest cathedrals, although much of the first cathedral was replaced during a turbulent medieval history.

The long nave, one of the longest in England, and the splendid processional way, or ambulatory, around the apse at the east end of the cathedral date from de Losinga's building, and it is highly likely that one of the first processions Norwich saw was to mark his funeral when in 1119 he was buried before the high altar of the church he had founded. It is likely too that the ancient effigy preserved in the ambulatory and dating from around that time represents him. De Losinga's successor carried on his work and throughout the twelfth and early thirteenth century building went on. The central tower was the highest tower built by the Normans in England.

Until the Reformation the cathedral was the centre of worship not only for the diocese but for a community of as many as sixty Benedictine monks, served and assisted by a vast staff – the Master of the Cellar alone had fifty men under his charge. The relationship between city and monastery was not always an easy one and in 1272 the Norman cloisters were much damaged during a riot when the towns-folk invaded the precincts, were repulsed by the abbot's forces and then forced their way in once more. The destruction was such that the church was reconsecrated in 1278 in the presence of Edward I and his queen, Eleanor. Extensive rebuilding was called for and the cloisters were not finally completed until 1430.

Riots were not the only causes of destruction. In 1362 a mighty wind blew down the spire and destroyed the Norman clerestory of the apse. Both were rebuilt by Bishop Thomas Percy (1355–69), brother of the powerful Earl of Northumberland.

In 1463 the spire fell again, struck by lightning,

which caused a huge fire. This too led to extensive rebuilding. From this reconstruction dates the beautifully vaulted nave – a lierne vault, one in which the main ribs are joined together by smaller ribs with bosses at each intersection. This was the work of Bishop Walter Lyhart and it was his successor, James Goldwell (1472–99), who was responsible for the present stone spire, 315 feet high and second only to Salisbury's among our cathedrals. Goldwell was a great builder and his embellishment of the apse is recorded by a series of gilded carvings of wells in the roof bosses above it, an example of the heraldic play on words known as a rebus. His effigy, decked in a marvellous cope, is the finest in the cathedral. In 1583 the monastery was dissolved and a new foundation established, the last prior, William Castleton, becoming the first dean. This was not the only link between the old order and the new. Because he was anxious to appropriate all the income enjoyed by the bishop and abbot, Henry VIII made the abbot of nearby St Benet's Abbey Bishop of Norwich. Thus, St Benet's Abbey was never officially dissolved, and so the Bishop of Norwich is technically still entitled to be regarded as a mitred abbot, a unique distinction among English bishops.

In common with most cathedrals Norwich was defaced and desecrated during the Civil War, but with the Restoration the city gave generously to repair what had been taken or spoilt, and Norwich did not suffer the same long sad period of decline as nearby Peterborough.

A painted roof boss in the cloister showing Henry II's penance at St Thomas's tomb.

During the second half of the last century, and throughout this one, affection and money has been lavished on the cathedral's restoration and today it is as well maintained as any in England, and far better presented than most. There is a well-designed Visitor Centre, with exhibitions illustrating the history and life of the cathedral, and a cinema showing a series of film and slide presentations which draw attention to Norwich's many treasures.

Among the most memorable and exciting are the

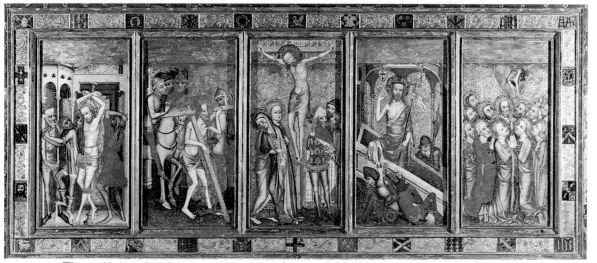

The retable in St Luke's Chapel. The greatest surviving masterpiece of medieval East Anglian art, it shows the betrayal and Crucifixion.

The high altar with the bishop's throne behind. The sanctuary has preserved its original plan, universal until 1100 and now being revived, in which Holy Communion is celebrated facing the people.

magnificent series of roof bosses. Binoculars are essential if one is to begin to appreciate these exquisite and carefully coloured examples of the medieval sculptor's art. There is a mirror trolley in the nave and by far the best way to study them is to train your binoculars on the mirror. Stories from the Old and New Testaments have never been more arrestingly or quaintly told. Among everyone's favourites is the Noah's Ark boss, a splendid reproduction of which, in the form of a paper-weight, is on sale in the cathedral shop.

There are fine bosses too in the fourteenth-century Bauchon Chapel, telling the tale of an empress falsely accused by her wicked brother who had tried to seduce her. In Norwich's splendid cloisters the bosses are much nearer to eye level and so easier to enjoy. Here we can see the Harrowing of Hell, the Crucifixion, the martyrdom of King Edmund and of St Thomas of Canterbury, and Henry II doing penance at St Thomas's tomb.

Also in the cloisters is one of those lovely and simple expressions of continuity which are such remarkable features of English cathedrals. Among the niches where medieval statues once stood are four familiar figures, inconspicuously but perfectly blending with their surroundings: George V and George VI, the two twentieth-century kings who loved Norfolk above all counties, together with their queens.

There are moving reminders of mortality, too. Close by the entrance to the cloister is an upright slab incised with a skeleton dating from the mid-sixteenth century. It carries the injunction:

> All you who do this place pass by
> Remember Death for you must die.
> As you are now, even so was I.
> As I am so shall you be.
> Thomas Gooding he do stay,
> Waiting for God's Judgement Day.

It is just possible that the man who saw as much change as anyone in this place was among the first to see this inscription. He was Osbert Parsley, whose own monument in the nave tells us that he became a member of the choir in 1535, singing the Latin services. He remained in office through the Dissolution and the reigns of Edward VI and Mary Tudor, and survived the first twenty-five years of Elizabeth's reign, dying in 1585.

Norwich has a small but well designed treasury in which an incomparable array of pre-Reformation silver from all over the diocese is displayed, together with fascinating captions which help the visitor realize the true purpose of these beautiful vessels. It is pointed out, for instance, that the enormous silver flagons were necessary because in 1673 the Test Act obliged all who would hold official positions to take communion on great festival days. Attention is drawn too to the knife marks on the pattens (the sacred vessels from which communion bread is

The arch over the door to the cloister, known as the Prior's Door.

distributed) showing where the bread was cut, and to the sifter spoons, which were needed to take the cork from the chalices after the Reformation, when the congregation was able to receive both bread and wine at communion for the first time.

Norwich has a fine set of misericords, some sadly damaged, and an unusual window, known as the Erpingham window, made up of a collection of medieval Norwich glass and placed in the north aisle in 1963. One of the most precious treasures of the cathedral is the retable, or altarpiece, brought from a Norwich church in 1958 and placed behind the altar in St Luke's Chapel. It tells the story of the betrayal and Crucifixion of Christ and is a work of rare genius.

St Luke's Chapel itself is yet another example of adaptability. Since 1564 it has been the official parish church of the Parish of St Mary in the Marsh, whose own church was demolished in that year.

Everywhere there is an atmosphere of well-ordered peace, best summed up in the famous words of Norwich's favourite saint, Julian of Norwich, one of the most remarkable Englishwomen of the Middle Ages: 'All shall be well, and all shall be well, and all manner of things shall be well.'

ROCHESTER

The Cathedral Church of Christ and St Mary

Cathedral and castle often stood close by each other in England's medieval cities but nowhere is this architectural representation of the two pillars of medieval society, God and Caesar, Church and State, seen to more dramatic effect than at Rochester from across the Medway. But there was a cathedral here long before the great Norman castle was built and it is a much loved church which today stands beside the ruins of the fortress.

Ecclesiastically and architecturally Rochester is overshadowed by its neighbour at Canterbury. Most of England's great medieval cathedrals are the mother church of large and important dioceses, but Rochester resembles the lesser cathedrals of France, where dioceses are smaller than in England and far more numerous. Though it has always been in Canterbury's shadow, and though today it is much

The Wheel of Fortune in a restored thirteenth-century wall painting.

altered and reconstructed, with its spire dating only from the early years of this century, Rochester is nevertheless a fine and important building and has a longer history than any cathedral in England save Canterbury.

Rochester, together with London, was one of the two sees founded by St Augustine in 604, just seven

The magnificent mid-fourteenth-century doorway which leads from the south-east transept to what is now the chapter-house.

*A fine overall view of the
cathedral from the west.*

years after he came to England and established his church in Canterbury. Its first bishop, Justice, was one of those sent by Pope Gregory in 601 to help the English mission.

Of the first cathedral, dedicated to St Andrew, patron saint of Augustine's own monastery in Rome, there is no trace, though during the restoration of 1889 some of its foundations were discovered by the west front and its apse is marked out in bronze in the nave. In that cathedral St Paulinus, apostle of the north, and Ithamar, the first native-born English bishop, were buried. By the time of the Norman Conquest, however, the cathedral, which had witnessed much strife and turmoil during the reigns of the Saxon kings, punctuated by Danish invasions, was, we are told, 'almost fallen to pieces with age'. The great Lanfranc, Archbishop of Canterbury, appointed Gundulph bishop, and he set about building a mighty castle at Rochester and a new cathedral, which, unlike the old, was to be the church of a Benedictine monastery.

Of Gundulph's early building only the crypt (later extended) survives, but in 1130 the new cathedral of St Andrew was consecrated in the presence of Henry I. Almost immediately a fire destroyed the city and damaged the church, though the nave survived and was incorporated in the present cathedral. Rochester's story reminds us just how vulnerable to fire those early medieval towns were, for there were further major fires in 1137 and 1179. Nevertheless the west front survives and, dating from the first half of the thirteenth century,

*The cathedral's most notable feature is the great west door
with its Norman arch and tympanum.*

the presbytery and east transept and choir. This was not an easy period, and in 1215, when Rochester was the centre of resistance for rebel bands holding out against the King, the castle besieged, and when it finally fell the cathedral invaded too. The chronicles tell us that 'Not a pyx was left in which the Body of the Lord might rest upon the altar'. Good Friday, 1264, saw the cathedral plundered and desecrated again, this time by the followers of Simon de Montfort in their civil war against Henry III.

The thirteenth century was a notable one in the cathedral's history. In 1201 a baker called William of Perth, known for his generosity to the poor, was murdered by his servant just outside Rochester. He was on a pilgrimage to the Holy Land. He was buried in the cathedral and soon there were stories of miracles occuring at his tomb, stories which the monks were anxious to encourage because they felt bypassed in every way by people flocking to the tomb of St Thomas of Canterbury. So a shrine was built to St William, as they called him, though he was never officially canonized, and for a time it was

indeed a place of pilgrimage and the pilgrims' offerings were used to adorn and enlarge the cathedral during the late thirteenth and the fourteenth centuries. The nave was completed and the central tower built, capped with a wooden spire. From this time, too, dates the first and greatest of the cathedral's glories, the supremely beautiful doorway leading to the chapter-house.

The decoration of the choir walls is also fourteenth-century. Much restored and considerably added to by Gilbert Scott during the restoration of the last century, these walls were first painted to commemorate Edward III's victories over the French. The cathedral was completed by the beginning of the sixteenth century. The nave, clerestory and great west window date from the last years of the fifteenth century and the Lady Chapel from the first decade of the sixteenth.

With the dissolution of the monasteries Rochester, in common with all our cathedrals, suffered change. A document of 1540 which records the surrender by the monks, says that they gave things up 'of their own free will'. But the establishment was a very small one by then and there were only thirteen monks to be pensioned off when Henry VIII refounded the cathedral with a new dedication – to Christ and the Blessed Virgin Mary.

Rochester played a small but significant part in the brief history of the Counter-Reformation in England for the body of Cardinal Pole, last Roman Catholic Archbishop of Canterbury, who died on the same night as his queen, Mary Tudor, lay in state here. His bier was 'covered with a cloth of black velvet, with a great cross of white satin over all the length and breadth of the same, in the midst of

The simple but splendid Norman nave.

which cross his Cardinal's hat was placed' before he was taken to Canterbury for burial.

In 1607 we get an insight into the problems facing those charged with maintaining ancient buildings in earlier times. The reports of a visitation note that though the cathedral was generally in a good state, repairs were needed weekly 'because of its antiquity'.

Rochester fared better than Canterbury during the Civil War. The Parliamentary soldiers, some of whom left their greatcoats in the crypt where they can still be seen, contented themselves with superficial vandalism, plucking down the altar rails, for instance, and leaving them for firewood for the poor. However, the cathedral was in a dilapidated state by the time of the Restoration, though when Samuel Pepys came here in April 1661 he remarked that it was 'now fitting for use, and the organ then attuning'.

There were systematic attempts to continue repairing and improving throughout the eighteenth century, when the roof was completely releaded.

The nineteenth century was one of constant activity and successive restorations were undertaken under the supervision of Lewis Cottingham and George Gilbert Scott and, finally, J. L. Pearson. The last major addition came in 1904 when a new spire – Rochester had been without one since 1825 – was put on the central tower. The restorations at Rochester were more sensitively carried out than in many churches and cathedrals, and today a visitor could appropriately echo the comments of a seventeenth-century tourist who, remarking on the 'little and sweet' city, said 'the cathedral, though . . . but small and plain, yet it is very lightsome and pleasant'.

Rochester is not as rich in treasures as our greater cathedrals but there is much to admire here, including the damaged but still noble and magnificent west door, massive and reassuring Norman columns in the nave, some thirteenth-century woodwork in the choir and – its chief glory – the unsurpassed carving around the fourteenth-century doorway to the chapter-house. There are two fine statues of Henry I and of Matilda and among the memorials the most splendid is undoubtedly that to Bishop John of Sheppey (1353–60) which survived in a remarkable state because it was walled up for two centuries. There is a memorial tablet to Dickens who lived nearby and a fine effigy of Dean Reynolds Hole who founded the National Rose Show. The most unusual and moving of all the memorials, however, are the medieval graffiti carved into the pillars of the crypt, in this case not to deface but to express a humble piety. They are an altogether fitting adornment to a church which takes English people back to the very roots of their faith.

The moving graffito scratched in the twelfth century on the walls of the crypt.

ST PAUL'S

The dome of St Paul's, rising confident and magnificent, dominates most of those eighteenth-century paintings of London's riverside which made the fortune of many a print-maker. Two centuries later, photographs of the dome amid the acrid smoke of the blitz were symbols of the nation's resistance. Today, newly cleaned and sparkling, it can be seen only in occasional gaps in the deformed skyline which those in charge of planning post-war London have allowed.

But though it no longer dominates in scale, the dome dwarfs in architectural grandeur everything

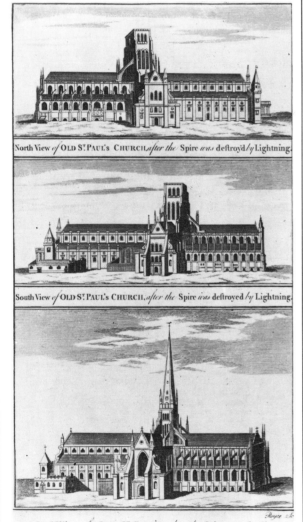

North View of OLD ST. PAUL'S CHURCH, after the Spire was deftroyd by Lightning.

South View of OLD ST. PAUL'S CHURCH, after the Spire was deftroyed by Lightning.

South View of OLD ST. PAUL'S, when the Spire was ftanding.

Old St Paul's, the largest Christian church
north of the Alps.

that has been erected round about. This is more than London's cathedral: it is the nation's church. Here in 1965 they brought the body of Churchill as they had brought those of Nelson and Wellington before. Here in 1977 the Queen came for the thanksgiving to mark the twenty-fifth anniversary of her accession, just as Queen Victoria had come for her great Diamond Jubilee eighty years earlier. Here, in 1981, in a London wild with excitement, the wedding of the Prince of Wales took place. Only Westminster Abbey has seen more pomp and ceremony, but the Abbey is essentially a royal church and also a Gothic church. St Paul's can almost claim the whole Commonwealth as its diocese and it is the only Renaissance cathedral in Britain.

This is the fifth cathedral on this site and there was almost certainly a church on Ludgate Hill before the Romans left Britain. The first cathedral was built shortly after Mellitus was consecrated Bishop of the East Saxons by St Augustine in 604, just seven years after the missionary saint had established his church at Canterbury.

Mellitus's wooden cathedral was burnt down within a century, and the first stone cathedral, built by St Erkenwald and later the site of his shrine and place of pilgrimage, was sacked and fired by the Vikings. The Saxon cathedral which replaced it at the end of the tenth century was destroyed by fire in 1087. It was after this that work began on a church which was to become the largest in England and one of the three greatest in Europe. Dedicated to St Paul and completed around the middle of the thirteenth century, it was 596 feet long. In 1315 it was given a spire that rose almost five hundred feet into the sky, the tallest ever built anywhere. Struck by lightning in 1444, the spire was replaced – only to be struck down again a century later.

Even without its spire Old St Paul's dominated Elizabethan London, but by then it was showing sad signs of neglect. Like all our English cathedrals it was sorely used during the period of the Commonwealth and the ascendancy of the Puritans. Its choir was used as a barracks for cavalry. Before the Civil War Inigo Jones had been employed on its restoration, and after 1660 a young man called Christopher Wren was asked to advise on how the huge but crumbling church could once again become a fitting cathedral for a great capital city.

The west front of Christopher Wren's new
St Paul's – its dome flanked by superb
baroque towers.

they included no traditional nave or aisles to the choir. As Barry found when he was commissioned to build a new Parliament after another fire nearly two centuries later, it is a soul-destroying task to work under a committee where all have ideas but few have any deep knowledge, and it was only the enlightened patronage of Charles II which saved Wren. He gave him a warrant which enabled him to deviate from his second, reluctantly approved, design by allowing the architect 'liberty in the prosecution of work, to make some variations, rather ornamental than essential, as from time to time he should see proper'. Today we can see in the cathedral the scale model of Wren's second design (first unveiled in 1673) and appreciate the variations he made.

Gunpowder and battering-rams were needed to demolish the ruins of Old St Paul's and it was not until 1675, nine years after the fire, that the first stone of the new cathedral was laid. Work began, as was the tradition with cathedrals, at the east end. In 1686 the foundations of the west front were laid and by 1697 the chancel was consecrated. Within another ten years the west towers were almost complete and the dome was finished in 1710. The following

He pondered the problem and proposed a dome, but before the debate could be resolved the city of London was engulfed in the great fire of September 1666. The fire is graphically recorded in Pepys' diary but the most succinct epitaph of Old St Paul's is found in the diary of John Evelyn: 'thus lay in ashes that most venerable church, one of the ancient masterpieces of early piety in the Christian world, beside near a hundred more.'

By 1666 the thirty-four-year-old Christopher Wren (son of the Dean of Windsor and nephew of Matthew Wren, successively Bishop of Hereford, Norwich and Ely) was already renowned as a mathematician and as an architect of genius. Professor of astronomy at the age of twenty-five, one of the founders of the Royal Society before he was thirty, architect of the Sheldonian Theatre at Oxford, he was unquestionably the foremost architect of his age when in 1669 he was charged with the task of building a new St Paul's.

A small part of the nave had survived the fire and there were many who wanted to rebuild from the gaunt and extensive ruins another Gothic church. Wren's first designs for a new cathedral capped by a dome were rejected by the Commissioners because

A shaft of sunlight penetrates the
interior of Wren's Renaissance
masterpiece.

*The dome of St Paul's, decorated by James Thornhill
with scenes from the life of St Paul – much admired
but done against the advice of the architect.*

year Parliament declared the building of St Paul's accomplished. It had taken thirty-five years and Wren was seventy-nine. He had fought a constant and exhausting battle. Two or three times a week he had been hauled up in a basket to the top of the scaffolding to examine the work – and all for £200 a year, £60 of which he gave back to the building fund. He had problems getting the right amount of stone from Portland, problems with finance, and problems with those who wanted to paint the inside of the dome. He himself never wanted it to be painted but rather to be encrusted with mosaic. Here he was defeated and James Thornhill painted the monochrome scenes from the life of St Paul which have always been much admired. In spite of that set-back, however, and obstacles which would have defeated many a lesser man, the building which emerged is without question one of the greatest in Europe. Its mastery of space and light is a supreme achievement. Aesthetically and architecturally it is more pleasing and successful than St Peter's in Rome, with which it is often compared. It is small wonder that Wren went back every year until his death at the age of ninety to sit under the dome; and appropriate that his simple memorial should carry the words: *Si monumentum requiris, circumspice* (If you seek his monument, look around you).

No major cathedral was ever built so quickly, but thirty-five years is a long space in the life of a man and Wren was anxious to see all accomplished in his lifetime. Though St Paul's has been altered and added to since 1711 this is still the church that Wren

designed. Here was a place to which people would come not on a personal pilgrimage to venerate some long dead saint but rather to express a sense of national identity, and so it was right that Wren should gather round him some of the most talented artists of the age to contribute to the creation of a national church. Some of their names, like those of the plasterers Doogoode and Wilkins and the carvers Francis Bird and the Kempsters, are now little known, but two men produced work of such extraordinary genius here that they are fit to be bracketed with Wren himself. They are Grinling Gibbons, who did some of his finest carving at St Paul's, and the Frenchman Jean Tijou, perhaps the most accomplished artist in wrought iron of all time. Recent cleaning has revealed much of Gibbons' work on the outside of St Paul's, but his greatest skills were displayed inside, where he designed and carved the choir stalls. Tijou was responsible for the sanctuary gates in the north and south choir aisles, for the altar rails, and other detailed work of great beauty such as the dean's staircase in the south-west tower.

But the glory of St Paul's is its dome. Wren, who was more influenced by the Gothic than many writers have given him credit for, was particularly inspired by the great lantern at Ely, where he himself was responsible for some of the restoration when his uncle, Matthew, was bishop there. The centre of his great church was to have a similar focal point of beauty, and in the dome of St Paul's Wren provided it.

Since Wren's death at the age of ninety in 1723, other artists have been employed to adorn St Paul's, and the cathedral has become in every sense the great national temple he envisaged. Many heroes have been laid to rest here and artists of great note employed to ensure that they had fitting memorials. Dominating the nave aisle is the enormous, triumphant monument to the Duke of Wellington. Thirteen thousand people came here for his funeral. His tomb is in the crypt, a massive sarcophagus of Cornish porphyry resting on a vast block of granite from Aberdeen. Nearby lies Nelson. After Trafalgar his body was brought back in a barrel of rum to be buried here, amid scenes of great mourning and solemnity. The King was anxious that he should have a fitting tomb and a great marble sarcophagus, which had been made for Cardinal Wolsey but never used because of his fall from grace, was discovered at Windsor. Among the many other tombs in the crypt, where there is now also a vast treasury of the

The choir facing east towards the magnificent baldacchino
consecrated in 1958.

The case of the organ, elaborately and beautifully carved.
Some of the work is by Grinling Gibbons.

The beautiful wrought iron gates of the sanctuary, designed by Jean Tijou.

cathedral's plate, are those of three of England's greatest painters: Reynolds, Lawrence and Turner.

Of all the statues in St Paul's the finest one created for this cathedral is Flaxman's of Nelson, but undoubtedly the most moving and impressive work of art in the whole cathedral is the one surviving piece of Old St Paul's: the effigy of John Donne (1573–1631), the most famous of all St Paul's deans. Poet, philosopher, priest, here he stands, a life-size figure by Nicholas Stone. We see him clothed in his own shroud in an effigy based on a portrait Donne put by his bed in his last days as a reminder of his mortality.

The national role of St Paul's and its importance as the Commonwealth's church is emphasized by two chapels: the beautiful Chapel of the Order of the British Empire (dedicated in 1960) and the Chapel of St Michael and St George – the chapel of the order which is conferred on those who have given distinguished service to their country or to the Commonwealth.

Some people will find the mosaic ceilings (the work of Sir William Richmond at the end of the last century) garish, but there are few who do not admire Holman Hunt's *Light of the World* in the south aisle, the artist's own copy of his masterpiece in Keble College, Oxford. The latest of the magnificent works of art in the cathedral was consecrated as recently as 1958 – the superbly decorated and ornate baldacchino above the high altar. It is made of English oak and is similar in form and spirit to what Wren himself wanted here. In the same year that the baldacchino was dedicated so too was the American Memorial Chapel, Britain's tribute to the 28,000 Americans based in Britain who lost their lives in the Second World War.

Thus, in its chapels, in its memorials to great heroes – as well as in its services – St Paul's continues to fill the role of a national church, but undoubtedly it owes its greatest fame to its beauty as one of the supreme architectural achievements of the world.

SALISBURY

The Cathedral Church of the Blessed Virgin Mary

The spire of Salisbury Cathedral has that power to challenge and to comfort which only the very greatest works of art possess. Whether you see it from miles away in the open country or from across the Avon (the view Constable immortalized), in sunshine or storm, at dusk or at daybreak, you will be strangely insensitive if you are not moved every time. To give orders of merit to great buildings is to

The purity of line of the uncluttered interior is seen to perfection in this view of the nave.

risk the wrath of man, but though Salisbury is not my favourite among English cathedrals, its spire is, for me, the most perfect single feature possessed by any of them.

If Salisbury's spire has the inevitable mystery of all objects of great beauty, the history of the cathedral is the least mysterious and best documented of all medieval cathedral histories and among the

most fascinating. It began outside the present city in 1070, when William the Conqueror disbanded his army at Sarum. An Iron Age hillfort, Sarum had become a Roman garrison and then, as Scarisbyrig, a major Saxon fortress. Its strategic importance was not lost on the Conqueror and as he sent his soldiers away so work began on one of England's most important Norman castles.

In 1075 the two dioceses of Sherborne and Ramsbury were amalgamated, given a new cathedral, and incorporated in the new diocese of Sarum. The castle was rebuilt and the cathedral extended by Bishop Roger, between 1102 and 1139. Roger was the most powerful man in the kingdom for many years, controlling the administration of the entire country. An obscure priest from Avranches in Normandy, he had been noticed by the king, Henry I, who was impressed by the speed with which he could say Mass. Chancellor, Justiciar, and Bishop of Salisbury at a time when Church and State were almost inseparable, Roger had such wealth and influence that his name was coupled with that of the King when royal commands were issued. He involved his family in government: his son (the clergy did not always keep their vows) was made Chancellor, his nephew became Bishop of Ely and treasurer and another nephew, Bishop of Lincoln. But they all fell from favour and were very harshly used when King Stephen took Sarum's castle during his war against Matilda. Within less than a century of Roger's death Sarum itself had begun its long decline into its present grassy-mounded oblivion, though until 1832 Old Sarum continued to return two Members to the unreformed House of Commons.

Today any visit to Salisbury really ought to begin at Old Sarum where we can see the ruins of the castle and trace the ground-plan of the old cathedral. It should then move on to Salisbury, and see what Bishop Richard Poore created there. For in 1217 he petitioned the Pope to build a new cathedral. In 1220 it was begun, with one of the canons from Old Sarum, Elias of Derham, supervising the work. Thirty-eight years later, in 1258, it was consecrated.

Wells is England's first wholly Gothic cathedral but Salisbury was the first to be built on an unencumbered site, its architects and designers

The Tower of Babel, one of the entertaining and elaborate carvings in the chapter-house.

being quite unconstrained by having to accommodate previous buildings or adapt and adopt to older ground-plans. Salisbury was also the only English cathedral, apart from St Paul's in the seventeenth-eighteenth centuries, to be built in one continuous operation. Wells certainly has great harmony, but Salisbury alone has the unity of a single composition, and it also has the most spacious and lovely close in England. Wells has more medieval buildings around it, but for sheer intrinsic architectural distinction no close can equal the buildings around Salisbury Cathedral, whether they date from the thirteenth century or, as in the case of the exceptional Mompesson House, from early in the eighteenth.

Bishop Poore was translated to Durham in 1228, just eight years after the Chapel of Holy Trinity and All Saints at the east end of the present cathedral had been dedicated. However, work went on without interruption or change and throughout its construction only two master masons were employed here, Nicholas of Ely and then Richard the Mason, who was responsible for the cloisters and the chapter-house.

Not everything was as we see it by 1258. There was still work to be done to the west front. That was finished in 1265. The cloisters, the earliest surviving in England, date from between 1263 and 1270. The chapter-house was being built simultaneously and was completed in 1284. The crowning glory, in

The central shaft of the chapter-house. It is almost certainly derived from that of Westminster Abbey.

Turner's view of the cathedral as seen through one of the windows of the cloister.

partly because of the attentions of 'improvers' in the last century. Nevertheless, Salisbury's austere interior has a beauty of its own. There is a purity of line here which is not found elsewhere. In spite of the restorers it is almost as Bishop Poore would have had us see it. The sweeping vista from the Trinity Chapel in the east to the west door is one of the finest interior views in any English cathedral.

Nothing in Salisbury's history matches the interest of the story of its building. It has never been in the mainstream of English history, like Winchester. It is not the burial place of kings and queens, nor have many of its bishops played any significant part in national affairs, though its medieval liturgy (the Sarum Rite) was widely taken as the model form of worship in pre-Reformation England.

During the Reformation it suffered less than most cathedrals, save for the wholesale destruction of what was probably among the very best of English stained glass. Even during the Civil War, when the cathedral was abandoned for a time, workmen were engaged to keep it in repair. There is an intriguing story of their being questioned as to who was employing them and their saying, 'Those who

Detail from Gabriel Loire's Prisoners of Conscience window.

every sense, was the spire and that was the result of a last-minute change of design. Originally Salisbury's tower was to have had a much squatter steeple.

The spire was built between 1285 and 1310: 404 feet high, the highest spire in England, and the second highest in Europe, it was constructed around an interior wooden scaffolding which still remains, as does the windlass which was used to haul up the stones from below. Inevitably it placed a great additional strain on the fabric, but that in itself was responsible for two of Salisbury's most distinctive internal features, the double or strainer arches at the entrance to the choir transept (in some ways reminiscent of the much larger scissor arches at Wells) erected late in the fourteenth century, and the stone girder arches added by Bishop Beecham in the fifteenth century.

Almost inevitably, after admiring the soaring majesty of the spire and the perfect proportions of the exterior, the visitor suffers a sense of disappointment on entering the cathedral, partly because of the dark appearance of the Chilmark limestone and

*Detail of the roof
of the nave.*

employed us will pay us; trouble not yourselves to enquire who they are. Whoever they are, they do not desire to have their names known.'

But if Salisbury had friends at Cromwell's Court, it suffered from a long period of sleepy neglect during the eighteenth century. Wren had been commissioned to strengthen the spire and supervise work after the Restoration and then a hundred years later Wyatt was called in. He destroyed the detached bell tower, and removed monuments, gravestones and chantry chapels, and much of what he did, such as taking away the old choir screen, must be regretted. But the chantry chapels were later additions, and removing the gravestones did give Salisbury the magnificent greensward setting which is one of its main delights.

In the nineteenth century George Gilbert Scott undid much of what Wyatt had done. Mercifully he strengthened the spire, although in 1950 it was discovered that the iron hoops which both he and Wren had used had rusted and major restoration was called for. At roughly the same time the choir screen installed in the nineteenth-century was taken away.

As a result of all this Salisbury's interior contains far fewer adornments than most cathedrals, but there are things of great beauty and interest. There is a superb thirteenth-century cope chest and a number of impressive tombs. The oldest is that of William Longespee, Earl of Salisbury. The bastard son of Henry I, he was one of the Magna Carta barons. He laid one of the foundation stones on 22 April 1220 and lies here today, a splendidly martial figure, on a wooden medieval tomb chest. Salisbury's most elaborate tomb is certainly the Earl of Hertford's. He, a Seymour, lies with his wife Lady Catherine Grey, sister of Lady Jane.

One of the four original copies of Magna Carta can be seen in the magnificent chapter-house, a building renowned in spite of Victorian restoration for some spirited medieval carving. Perhaps the most moving of all Salisbury's treasures, however, is its most recent: the Prisoner of Conscience Window in the Trinity Chapel. This jewel of stained glass, designed by Gabriel Loire at his studios near Chartres and dedicated in 1980, is an extraordinary blend of contemporary message with eternal truth. It is fitting that in this perfect building – a perfection that is beautifully captured in a plaster model of the cathedral, dating from 1825 – there should be such a harmonious and powerful twentieth-century work of art.

WELLS

The Cathedral Church of St Andrew

Wells has been called the queen of cathedrals. It has a matchless grace, a truly calm and quiet beauty. It does not dominate its surroundings like Durham or command a city set on a hill like Lincoln, but no cathedral has a more tranquil or harmonious setting. Around the mother church are the buildings which have housed those who have served it and ruled the diocese since the Middle Ages. There are other lovely cathedral precincts, but nowhere in England can we see so many medieval church buildings still fulfilling their ancient purpose. Nor is any great church closer to the countryside. Walk along the pathway to the end of the moat which surrounds and protects the Bishop's Palace, and to one side you have the cathedral and ancient city, to the other, green fields and open country. There is a peace about it all which makes us forget the original defensive reason for the moat and which contrasts sharply with the turbulent religious politics of powerful prelates who, in the eleventh and twelfth centuries, struggled fiercely to champion the claims first of Wells, then of Bath and then of Glastonbury to be the seat of the bishop.

Tradition has it that the first church here was

The cathedral from the east reflected in the placid waters of the moat around the Bishop's Palace.

founded by St Aldhelm, Saxon Bishop of Sherborne, early in the eighth century. Its dedication, to St Andrew, survived, as did its status as a college of secular clergy – there was never a monastery here, even when the first Saxon see of Wells was created in 909. But nothing of that first church remains, nor of the subsequent Norman cathedral built by Bishop Robert of Lewes (1136–66), save perhaps the font. It was this Robert who sought to rescue Wells from the oblivion thrust upon it by his predecessor John de Villula, who in 1088 had persuaded William II to make him Abbot of Bath and who had then made the church there the cathedral of his diocese.

Bishop Robert laid it down that henceforth the bishop was to be styled Bishop of Bath and Wells and his election was to be confirmed by both Chapters, but it was not until early in the thirteenth century that the dispute was finally settled by the Pope. Since then all bishops of Somerset have been so styled. In the intervening years there was even one period under Bishop Savaric, who coveted Glastonbury and its many romantic and holy associations, when the see was known as 'Bath and Glastonbury'. To this day Wells comes second after Bath in the bishop's title, though since the dissolution of Bath Abbey in 1539 there has been only one Chapter capable of electing a bishop and one church in which his chair could be placed. In spite of all this ecclesiastical backbiting, there rose at Wells between the end of the twelfth and the middle of the fifteenth century one of the most unified in conception and execution of all Europe's great cathedrals.

The building we see today was begun by Bishop Reginald de Bohun about 1175, and his plan was so faithfully followed and carefully adapted by his successors over the next two and a half centuries that there are no incongruous or jarring features. It was the first entirely Gothic cathedral, with pointed arches throughout. Even the stone that was used came throughout the period from a single quarry at Doulting, eight miles away, a quarry that is still worked for the cathedral today.

Consecrated in 1242, the cathedral was virtually complete, save for the cloisters, by the end of the fourteenth century: a building remarkable for its

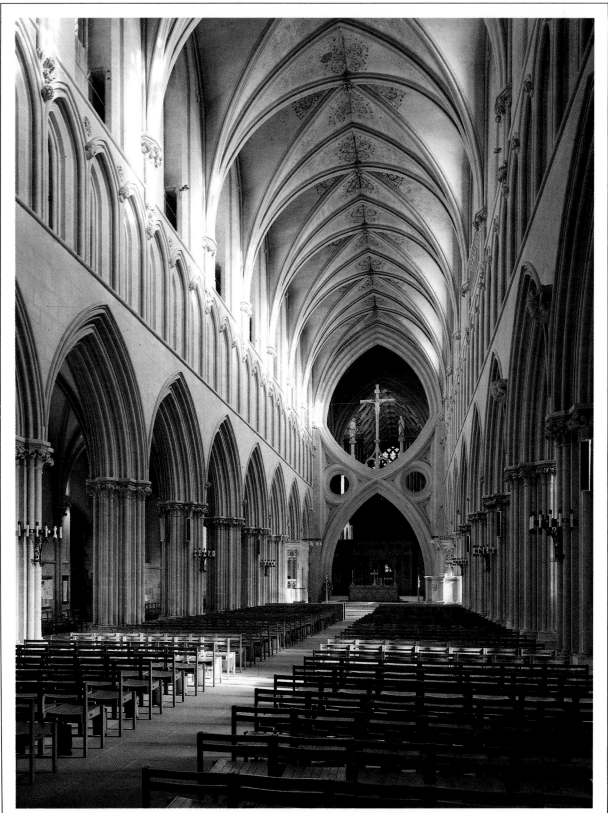

The nave, looking east towards the scissor arches, the cathedral's most distinguishing internal feature and an ingenious answer to a structural problem.

The west front – the finest medieval sculpture gallery in England, though some of the original statues have recently been replaced during extensive restoration.

restrained and elegant enrichment, though there are delightful touches of exuberance, as in the magnificent carved capitals.

To the twelfth and thirteenth centuries we owe the transept, the nave, west front and chapter-house; to the fourteenth, the Lady Chapel, the central tower, the retrochoir and reconstructed choir, the inverted arches in the crossing and the south-west tower. Then in the fifteenth century the cloisters were built and the central tower altered, and today Wells still looks much as it did a hundred years before the Reformation.

It has, of course, suffered from the vandalism of the zealous and the bigoted, the over-lavish attentions of Victorian restorers, and, most of all, the ravages of time. There was the habitual smashing of images and glass at the time of the Reformation, and again during the Civil War, and Wells had its own particular problems even after that because the whole of Somerset was in turmoil in 1685. During the abortive Monmouth rebellion of that year the cathedral was used for the stabling of horses by the rebel forces, who used the lead from the roof for bullets, and even broached a barrel of beer on the high altar. There is a graphic description of this wanton destruction and desecration in Conan Doyle's *Micah Clarke*. Little happened in the eighteenth century but in the nineteenth came the restorers. Much of what they did was good: layers of whitewash were removed, an attempt was made to restore original decoration and colouring, and for the first time attention was devoted to the west front.

It is the west front that is Wells's surpassing glory, without question the finest medieval sculpture gallery in the country – over two hundred superb examples of the genius of truly accomplished artists. Recently their wonderful carvings have been the subject of controversy, for in the massive restoration that has been needed to save the west front it was soon discovered that some of the statues had deteriorated beyond repair or recognition. The decision was taken to replace a few of them with new statues. The whole story of the project is beautifully told in a series of photographs in the cathedral, though there are still those who will argue that restoration should not have extended to replacement, but merely to keeping in an architectural aspic what time and the weather had been pleased to preserve.

We can get some idea of the crispness and beauty which must once have stunned anyone approaching the west front if we look at some of the carved capitals in the south transept. Quite unlike anything in any other English cathedral, they are a vivid stone tableau of medieval life. The most famous series is that known as the fruit stealers, a comic-strip-like narrative of the catching of an orchard thief. On another pillar is a man with toothache and it is obviously more than coincidence that there are eleven carvings of our medieval ancestors with this affliction in a cathedral whose most pious medieval bishop – the second Bishop Bitton – was venerated

St George slays the Dragon,
one of the misericords
in the choir stalls.

as a saint and held accountable for a number of miraculous cures of tooth trouble.

Wells's most famous unique feature – and it probably has more such rarities than any other English cathedral – is the celebrated scissor arches. Like vast jawbones of whales they dominate any view down the nave, but are perhaps seen to best advantage from the south-east corner of the transept. They are the ingenious answer of the medieval master mason, William Joy, to the alarming cracks in the masonry which appeared in 1338, after the central tower was raised. He inserted these arches two years later as additional supports for the tower and to spread the weight on the foundations, a function they have performed effectively for over six centuries.

The choir stalls, relics of the Victorian restorers, are disappointing, but there is a set of sixty misericords which are among the very finest in existence, and the stalls have been beautifully adorned by a series of needlework panels and banners, worked between 1927 and 1948. There is fine glass too, the great Jesse window (depicting Christ's descent from David) in the east and also a series of kaleidoscopic windows of medieval fragments assembled from glass smashed in the sixteenth and seventeenth centuries. There is a set of seven splendid effigies of Saxon bishops in the choir aisle, all carved at the end of the twelfth century and housing the bones of the bishops who knew the earlier Saxon cathedral as their home. Among the more recent effigies those of John Drokensford

most beautiful of all chapter-houses. Reached by a noble stairway, it is an exquisitely proportioned octagon. Here we can see where the secular canons who governed Wells, each from a different part of the diocese, had their prebendal seats. Many of these men were at best irregular in their attendances, and so they had deputies, or vicars, to perform their offices for them, and in the mid-fourteenth century Bishop Ralph of Shrewsbury saw to it that these vicars had suitable housing on the premises. Today we can still walk from the chapter-

The beautiful stone staircase to
the chapter-house and
vicar's hall.

(1309–29) and Thomas Bekynton are especially magnificent. Bekynton's is one of those wonderful double tombs, the bishop resplendent in his finery above and the skeleton remains below. It was apparently erected, with its constant reminder of the fading glories of the world, some fourteen years before he died in 1465. And there is a magnificent lectern with an inscription recording that this 'brazen deske' was given by Dr Robert Creyton on return from the exile he shared with Charles II.

No one dare write about Wells without mentioning the fourteenth-century clock, one of the two earliest surviving clocks in the country, the other being at Salisbury. The original works of this one are now in the Science Museum in London but every quarter of an hour we see the quaint figure of Jack Blandiver kicking the quarters with his heels, and then a roundabout of knights on horseback, one being unseated at each turn. Naturally the whole thing has been restored through the centuries but apparently the last major restoration was as long ago as 1727.

Wells not only has the finest west front and most magnificent carved capitals, it also has one of the two

The superbly proportioned
octagonal chapter-
house.

house through the Vicar's Hall, across the stone bridge above the Chain Gate, and down into Vicar's Close, the best-preserved medieval street in England. In this series of stone houses, fronting a cobbled street, with a delightful chapel at the end, the priest and lay vicars still live. It is all in homely contrast to the great building on the other side of the cathedral, the moated and turreted Bishop's Palace, itself still the residence of the Bishop of Bath and Wells, a fitting home for a bishop whose office has carried with it ever since the reign of Richard I the right of being one of the sovereign's two principal supporters at the coronation.

WINCHESTER

The Cathedral Church of the Holy Trinity, St Peter, St Paul and St Swithun

The tomb of William Rufus in the choir. He was killed while hunting in the New Forest.

There is nothing spectacular about Winchester Cathedral – until you go inside. It sits squat, low and unspectacular, so modest that it successfully disguises its own vast size. For this is the longest Gothic church in Europe. Of the ancient churches of Christendom only St Peter's in Rome is longer, and there is no more surprising or stunning vista than the one that greets you as you look east, down the gloriously vaulted and beautifully proportioned nave, towards the choir screen and the high altar beyond. For a better and more unusual view climb the stairs above the west door to the treasury, itself well worth a visit, and pause for a moment to absorb the atmosphere of a church that contains the bones of some of England's earliest kings; the grand tombs of the grandest of medieval bishops; the simple grave of one of the greatest English novelists; and the memorial to that very special workman whose

courageous devotion at the beginning of this century saved it all.

This is the third cathedral in Winchester's long and proud history. In 635 King Kynegils of Wessex was baptized in this his capital city and the Anglo-Saxon Chronicle of 648 records, 'In this year was built a Church at Winchester which King Cenwalh made and consecrated in St Peter's name'. This became the first cathedral church of Wessex. Nothing remains of it, nor of the next, and greater, Saxon cathedral which housed the tomb of Bishop Swithun whose name was incorporated in its dedication, as it is in that of the present cathedral. The humble Swithun would not be buried within his church and when his grave was opened on 15 July 971, so that his bones could be borne inside, the heavens, we are told, wept for forty days.

The bones of many early Saxon kings and bishops, together with those of the Danish King Canute and his queen, Emma – great benefactors to Winchester – are still here, contained in mortuary chests which rest on top of the screens around the presbytery.

Even though Wessex was submerged in the new Norman kingdom of England, Winchester remained one of the two principal cities of the land throughout the Norman period. Indeed for the

The chantry chapel of William Wykeham, the most notable of all Winchester's episcopal builders.

Winchester, the longest Gothic church in Europe, seen here from the south-west.

whole of the Middle Ages the great diocese of which this cathedral was the centre was the richest in the country, stretching as it did from the south coast to the south bank of the Thames in London.

It was the first of the Norman bishops, Bishop Walkelin (who succeeded the Anglo-Saxon Stigand in 1070), who began to build a new cathedral in which St Swithun's bones were given a new and beautiful shrine. We can get some idea of the massive but simple dignity of that Norman cathedral if we go to the north and south transepts where the rough-hewn Norman masonry, and the strong and simple arches, remain virtually unchanged. The Norman cathedral, far bigger than Durham and Peterborough, was probably the largest Romanesque church in Europe. In it Richard de Bernay, second son of William the Conqueror, was buried. He was killed at the age of sixteen, gored by a stag in the New Forest. William's third son, William Rufus, who succeeded him as William II was buried here too, after he was shot while hunting in the same forest.

A simple slab in the choir stalls marks William Rufus's grave today. He was regarded as such an inveterate enemy of the Church and its faith that devout men thought the heavens protested at his being given a Christian burial in such a holy place. Be that as it may, in 1107, seven years after his death, the great tower of the cathedral collapsed and the transepts had to be rebuilt.

The cathedral we know – and there is no more magnificent Gothic church in Europe – was largely inspired by the most powerful and famous of all the Bishops of Winchester, William of Wykeham (1367–1404) and his master mason, William Wynford. To them we owe the lofty Perpendicular arches of the nave with their elegant balconies and clerestory above. They make the whole nave a tunnel of light.

Appropriately, William of Wykeham rests in a superb chantry chapel in the nave, angels guarding his head and clerks sitting at his feet. This and the other chantry chapels are the most important additions to the cathedral since William of Wykeham's great rebuilding. In the middle of the retrochoir is the lavish and ornate chantry of Cardinal Beaufort, resplendent in his red hat. Four times Lord Chancellor of England, he was mainly responsible for the condemnation of Joan of Arc, and in 1923, after her canonization, the statue of the young French peasant warrior-saint was placed opposite her accuser's tomb.

Among the other chantry chapels are those of William of Wayneflete, another mighty prelate,

The nave looking east towards the chancel,
a tunnel of light.

*The sanctuary gates
in the south
choir.*

bishops waited to greet him at the great west door. With crosses raised and censers swinging, clerics who had been appalled at the breach with Rome went in solemn procession to the high altar, leading a man whom they looked upon as God's chosen instrument to restore the True Faith to England. The Queen, we are told, blazed with jewels so that 'the eye was blinded as it looked upon her; her dress was of black velvet flashing with gems and a splendid mantle of Cloth of Gold fell from her shoulders; and through the Mass which followed the marriage service she never took her eyes off the Crucifix upon which they were devoutly fixed.' It must indeed have seemed a miraculous day for those who had watched with horror when, after Henry

*The retrochoir with its medieval
tiled floor, the most extensive
in England.*

Lord Chancellor of England, founder of Magdalen College, Oxford, and Provost of Eton. A central figure in English history throughout the fifteenth century, he negotiated with Jack Cade in 1450 and secured the release of Henry VI from the Tower of London in 1470.

One of the most interesting chantry chapels is that of Bishop Fox. Where, blind and infirm, he used to sit listening to the singing of the offices, we can see today the stone effigy of his decomposing corpse. There is also a chantry to Bishop Stephen Gardiner. He played the central role in one of Winchester's most glorious ceremonies when he officiated at the marriage of Mary Tudor and Philip of Spain in 1554. The chair on which the Queen sat is still in the cathedral. Few people today realize that for four years the king who was to send the Armada was King of England. Had it not been for Mary's early death the marriage which made him so would have been the most important dynastic union in English history. The ceremony that marked it was suitably impressive. Before the Nuptial Mass, 'as solemnly sung as at Toledo', a group of mitred

VIII had dissolved the monasteries, the Benedictines had been ejected from Winchester and the cathedral had been vandalized. St Swithun's shrine, for four centuries second only in importance to that of St Thomas à Becket, had been pillaged and shorn of all its precious stones and ornaments.

But there was to be no new shrine. Within five years Mary was dead and Philip became an implacable foe of England's new queen, having failed to win her hand too. Winchester suffered greatly from the bigoted attentions of its reforming bishop, Bishop Horne, during the reign of Elizabeth. He pulled down the chapter-house, and ruthlessly ravaged many of the most beautiful treasures of the cathedral. More destruction was to come during the Civil War. One commentator has it that 'the brass torn from the violated monuments' in 1644 'might have built a house as strong as the brazen towers of old romances'. Providentially, one of the Parliamentarian generals was a descendant of William of Wykeham and so his chantry at least remained undisturbed.

Though still a notable centre of scholarship, the city of Winchester has not been at the centre of our national life since the Civil War. Perhaps the most interesting events that happened here in the cathedral in the two centuries after that were two burials, of Izaak Walton in 1683 and Jane Austen in 1817. Jane Austen's grave is in the north aisle and is one of the most visited of all the memorials in the cathedral and one of the most felicitously worded. It records how 'the benevolence of her heart, her sweetness of temper, and the extraordinary endowments of her mind, obtained the regard of all who knew her, and the warmest love of her intimate connections'. This simple black slab is in marked contrast to the grand medieval and Tudor tombs and to a most fascinating Victorian one, the remarkably flamboyant effigy of Bishop Samuel Wilberforce, son of the great William, who lies in state in the south transept surrounded by kneeling angels.

At the beginning of the century it was discovered that the cathedral needed to be under-pinned: it had, in effect, been built on a great raft of timbers resting on a bed of peat. Originally the cost of restoration was estimated at £3,000 but by the time the work was accomplished, after seven years, in 1912, the bill had mounted to £113,000. The hero of the episode was a diver, William Walker. He had to work in fourteen feet of water and his exploits captured the imagination of his contemporaries. There is a memorial to him in the cathedral recording that he handled 25,800 bags of concrete and 114,900 concrete blocks as he replaced the peat. During the restoration, buttresses were added and five hundred tons of grouting and sixteen-and-a-half tons of tie-rods were used to strengthen the building. Much of the work was under one of Winchester's greatest treasures, the tiles of the retrochoir, the finest medieval floor in England.

Amongst the cathedral's other treasures are the square black basalt Norman font from Tournai in Belgium adorned with scenes from the life of St Nicholas, and the pre-Reformation choir pulpit. Even more important are the series of wall paintings in the Chapel of the Holy Sepulchre. Dating from the first quarter of the thirteenth century, they are among the best in Europe. There are more wall paintings in the Lady Chapel, though these have been altered and restored. They illustrate a series of miracles attributed to the Virgin, and among the most arresting is that which tells the story of how the Virgin came to the aid of a painter whose scaffolding had been knocked down by the devil because he painted him as an ugly creature. The east window of the Lady Chapel also warrants more than a passing glance, not for its quality but for its depiction of two kneeling queens – Elizabeth, wife of Henry VII, and, most unusually, Queen Victoria at the time of her Golden Jubilee.

So rich are its furnishings and so varied its treasures that there is a danger of thinking of Winchester merely as a great ecclesiastical museum. Two things in particular disproved this on my last visit. At four o'clock one of the clergy called the people to reflect on the true purpose of the cathedral as he said a brief prayer, and then, as I was coming out by the west door, I saw on the case containing the Book of Remembrance a little bunch of withering flowers, placed there by a Winchester woman a few days previously in memory of a brother killed in September 1916. The two events, perhaps insignificant in themselves, underlined the continuing purpose of this remarkable place.

The tomb of William of Wykeham. Though he is at peace, his clerks are still alert at his feet.

WORCESTER

The Cathedral Church of Christ and St Mary

There is no image more quintessentially English than that of Worcester Cathedral reflected in the broad and tranquil waters of the Severn and overlooking the most beautiful county cricket ground in the country. Though it is an almost perfectly proportioned cathedral, the enchantment lent by distance to the view fades somewhat on close inspection. It was not without reason, although with some exaggeration, that a guide book published at the turn of the century referred to the nineteenth-century restoration of Worcester as 'probably the most complete and far-reaching undergone by any British cathedral'. Nevertheless the proportions were not disturbed, the beauty of the tower was not impaired, and the interior, though itself much altered and 'improved' by A. E. Perkins and George Gilbert Scott, is still strikingly lovely. And no cathedral has a more fascinating history.

Though this is an Early English cathedral re-worked by the Victorians, it stands on one of the most ancient sites of English Christianity. The diocese of Worcester was established in 680 when the first cathedral, dedicated to St Peter, was consecrated, served by a group of missionaries who had come from St Hilda's Abbey at Whitby. It was a community which survived without flourishing for three troubled centuries until in 961 Bishop Dunstan, who was later translated to Canterbury, and his successor, Oswald, refounded the cathedral as the centre of a new Benedictine monastery dedicated to the Blessed Virgin Mary, again on the site of the present cathedral. For six hundred years Worcester served as both abbey church and cathedral.

There is no trace of Oswald's cathedral, but his great piety led to his canonization soon after his death. His tomb, venerated as a shrine, quickly became a place of pilgrimage. In 1041 Worcester was pillaged by the Danes but in 1062 acquired another saintly bishop in Wulstan, the prior of the abbey. He was the only one of the Saxon bishops to

The cathedral with its graceful central tower rising above the Severn,
a sight familiar to generations of cricket lovers.

The Norman crypt with its many aisles is one of the most interesting and extensive in England.

remain long in office after the Norman Conquest. In due course he too was canonized and so Worcester acquired a second shrine. Wulstan was a great builder and part of the cathedral he created still remains, most notably the crypt, the largest Norman crypt in England, in which he erected a magnificent new shrine to St Oswald with an ambulatory around the east end round which the pilgrims could file.

Wulstan's cathedral suffered much during the twelfth century, first from a fire in 1113 and then, in 1139, during the civil war of Stephen's reign, when the city was sacked. In the words of the monastic chronicler Florence of Worcester, 'as the enemy were rushing in from one gate to the other' the monks 'bore the relics of Oswald, our most gentle patron, out of the church'. In 1175 the tower fell and in 1180 there was yet another fire.

In 1203 Wulstan was canonized and shortly afterwards Worcester had a stroke of royal good fortune. In spite of the fact that the city took sides against King John, he decided that he would be buried in this cathedral. So it was that his body was brought here from Newark in October 1216 and buried before the high altar between the tombs of Oswald and the recently canonized Wulstan. Thus one of the least attractive medieval monarchs came to rest between two saints.

Two years later, in 1218, in the presence of King Henry III and most of the leading prelates and nobles of the land, the cathedral church of Worcester was dedicated to Mary and Peter, Oswald and Wulstan.

Most of the cathedral as the Victorians found it and essentially as we still see it dates from the thirteenth and fourteenth centuries. Throughout this period building continued, though there was a lull in the middle of the fourteenth century, roughly coinciding with the period of the Black Death. The choir and retrochoir date from the end of the thirteenth century. Most of the nave was built between 1317 and 1324 and it was finished between 1360 and 1374. The vaults and the west front were added at the end of the fourteenth century and at about the same time the chapter-house (built at the beginning of the twelfth century) was revaulted and embellished with a new door and windows.

Major building work at Worcester ended with the erection of the cloisters during the first forty years of the fifteenth century, the only later addition being one of the cathedral's most glorious and fascinating adornments and its second great royal tomb, the chantry chapel of Prince Arthur. Historians will always speculate on how different the course of English history might have been if Henry VII's first son, named after the legendary English king, had survived. But Arthur died at Ludlow in 1502 when only fifteen, shortly after contracting one of the most important dynastic marriages in English history, to Catherine of Aragon. The marriage was so important that the new Prince of Wales and heir, Henry, was quickly betrothed to the young widow. Arthur's body was brought from Ludlow to Worcester, and here in the cathedral a chantry was erected at the side of the high altar to contain his tomb. Not surprisingly, the chantry was spared the destructive purges of those who came, on King Henry's orders, after the monastery was dissolved to destroy the shrines of Oswald and Wulstan.

The tomb of King John, the earliest royal effigy in England. It dates from the thirteenth century and stands in the choir.

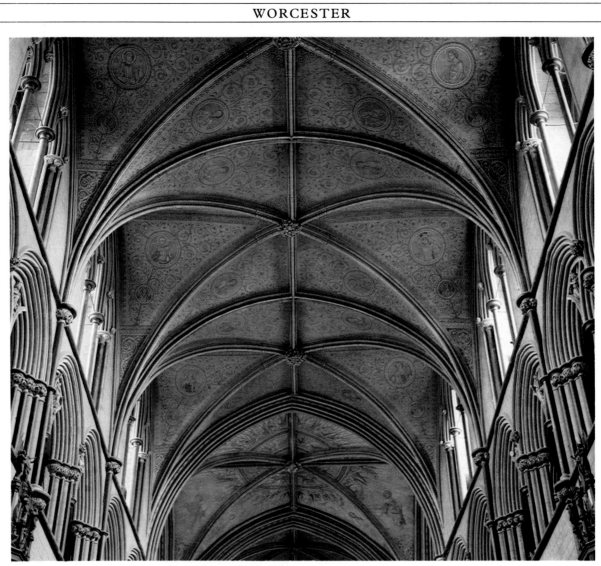

*Roof paintings in the choir which date from Worcester's
major restoration in Victorian times.*

Worcester was refounded as a cathedral by Henry VIII, and the last prior, Henry Holbeach, became the first dean. At this time the pulpitum was destroyed, the monks' stalls ripped out, statues broken and glass smashed. Further havoc was wrought during the troubles of the seventeenth century, when the city was faithful to the Royal cause. The Parliamentary army took possession in 1642 and the soldiers 'visited the cathedral where after every sort of vulgar abuse and wanton destruction that could be effected on its altar, which they pulled down, and its vestments and furniture, which they destroyed, the vault beneath it was explored and considerable treasure of stores and provision was discovered in it, supposed to have been sent thither from the col-legians of Oxford . . . for the use of the Royalists.'

Worcester suffered more than most in the Civil Wars because it was at the battle outside the city in 1651 that Charles II made a brave but abortive attempt to regain his throne. He fled, and after a series of remarkable adventures (including the famous episode in the oak tree) went into exile until his restoration in 1660. But six thousand prisoners were taken and 'penned up in the cathedral', and the Parliamentary army gave way to 'the most atrocious acts of outrage that the meanness of rapacity could stimulate in the dark mind of a sanguinary puritan; and although an ostensible authority for a general pillage was not absolutely given by Cromwell, it is as certain that not the least restraint was put upon the brutal violence of his ruffian troups, who fell to ravaging and plundering without mercy, few or none of the devoted citizens escaping their cruelty.'

It is not surprising that there was much need of restoration early in the eighteenth century, and Worcester was subject to more attention during that period than most other cathedrals. It was a haphazard attention, however, which made great use of whitewash, and it was not until 1857 that 'the great restoration' of the cathedral began, first under the auspices of A. E. Perkins and then of Sir George Gilbert Scott. Much of the cathedral was refaced, a process made necessary by the decay of the local sandstone but one which totally removed the patina of age. Inside, the cathedral was completely re-paved, windows were replaced and a new west door, nave, pulpit and choir screen, bishop's throne and reredos were installed. By the time the restored cathedral was reopened on 8 April 1874 well over £100,000, a vast sum in Victorian times, had been lavished on it, mainly by local benefactors.

Mercifully the crypt remains much as it was in Wulstan's day and nothing can detract from the glory of the nave with its two western bays dating from the very end of the twelfth century, and the rest, completing one of the finest Gothic naves, built in those two bursts punctuated by the Black Death in the following hundred years. The clerestory is bright and elegant, the vaulting of high quality and in the eastern transept and the Lady Chapel the shafts of Purbeck marble are especially beautiful. Arthur's chantry ranks with the best work of the early sixteenth century and although the chapter-house was gothicized, Norman work of great importance was preserved.

Among the cathedral's individual treasures are some magnificent misericords dating from around 1380, which include a complete set of the occupations of the months. Jutting into the cathedral, in the north choir aisle, is a fascinating stone window, a reminder that the sacrist's house was once here. From this place he could watch over the shrines of St Oswald and St Wulstan. Of those shrines there is no trace, nor do we know where their bones were scattered, but the tomb of the king who chose to lie between them is still here. Though the base dates from the fifteenth century the effigy itself, the lid of the original coffin, dates from around 1240 and is almost certainly the earliest royal effigy in England. It shows King John flanked by figures of Oswald and Wulstan. Among Worcester's other tombs the most fascinating is that of Sir John and Lady Beauchamp, which dates from the end of the fourteenth century. Sir John, steward of Richard II's household, was beheaded on a trumped up charge of treason in 1388.

There are fine tombs from much later times too, especially the Moore monument of 1613 and the magnificent monument to Bishop Hough completed by Roubiliac in 1743. Among the smaller treasures, the statues in Prince Arthur's chantry, a late fifteenth-century Virgin and Child in Nottingham alabaster, and the roof bosses in the cloister are perhaps the most notable.

The Victorian work here is of a high order, and there are touching reminders of two of those who loved Worcester most in this century. Beneath the west window is a simple stone marking the burial place of the ashes of Stanley Baldwin, and in the north wall is the Elgar window. Illustrating the Dream of Gerontius, it commemorates the most English of English composers who, though a Roman Catholic, loved this cathedral above all others.

The chantry of Prince Arthur, elder brother of Henry VII. He was brought here after his death at Ludlow in 1502.

YORK

The Cathedral and Metropolitical Church of St Peter

York owes its grandiloquent title to the fact that this is the cathedral church not only of the diocese of York but also of the northern province of England, the seat of one of our two archbishops. But it is as York Minster that everyone knows it, this largest of all the English Gothic cathedrals. I have known it since early childhood but it was not until 1972, when I came to see the astonishing results of the most massive cathedral-rescue operation ever undertaken in England, that I first saw it without scaffolding in its full glory. I realized then that this huge church was indeed the worthy centre of a city that had once dominated the whole of the north of England and is still by far the most interesting of ancient English towns.

The history of York was for well over a thousand years very much the history of northern England. Eboracum was one of the Romans' principal cities and fortresses. Here two Roman emperors died and here in 306 Constantine was proclaimed Caesar. He was the first of the Roman emperors to become a Christian and eight years later, in 314, a bishop from York attended one of the early councils of the Church at Arles. Towards the end of the fourth century the legions departed and the long night of the Dark Ages settled over the north of England.

The north side of York Minster, showing the conical roof of the chapter-house, from the city walls.

Then on the eve of Easter in 627 Edwin of Northumbria was baptized in York by Paulinus, who had come from Kent with Ethelburgha, the princess Edwin married. Pope Gregory himself decreed that York should be the church's missionary centre in the north and so it was appropriate that the minster, or missionary church, should be dedicated to St Peter. Thus the see of York was established within thirty years of St Augustine's mission to Canterbury, and for almost eight hundred years the archbishops of York disputed with those of Canterbury for supremacy in the English church. Finally the quarrel was resolved by Pope Innocent VI, in the fourteenth century, when he decreed that the Archbishop of York was to be Primate of England but that the Archbishop of Canterbury was to be Primate of *All* England. It was an Archbishop of York, Aeldred, who crowned William the Conqueror in Westminster Abbey, and so bitterly did the quarrel flare, in spite of pronouncements in Canterbury's favour, that in 1176 there was a ludicrous scene when the Archbishop of Canterbury sat on the right of the Papal Legate and the Archbishop of York, refusing to yield precedence, sat on Canterbury's lap. When the quarrel was finally determined by Innocent VI it was settled that each archbishop should carry his cross erect in the diocese of the other, but that the Archbishop of York should send a golden image to the shrine of St Thomas of Canterbury. Thus, says the seventeenth-century historian Fuller, 'when two children cry for the same apple, the indulgent father divides it betwixt them; and yet so that he giveth the bigger and better part to the child that is his darling.'

Of the early churches on this site we have little knowledge, only some evidence of their foundations as a result of recent excavation, but we do know that York was a great centre of learning in the eighth century, long before the Conquest, when the English scholar Alcuin was adviser to Charlemagne, the Holy Roman Emperor. William the Conqueror reckoned that York was so important that he appointed as his first Norman archbishop Thomas of Bayeux. It was Thomas who drew up a set of rules for the governing of the secular, or non-monastic, cathedrals which was the basis for the government of all such establishments. We can see some of the foundations of Thomas's cathedral, one of the greatest Romanesque buildings north of the Alps, but nothing remains above ground, although there

A skyline of towers and pinnacles. The flying buttresses were an unnecessary reinforcement as the nave was vaulted in wood rather than stone.

are a few fragments of glass which probably date from the Norman cathedral and which are incorporated in windows in the north of the nave and in the south clerestory windows.

During the twelfth century York acquired its saint, William Fitzherbert, first appointed archbishop in 1143 and reinstated after a dispute ten years later. The present minster was begun in 1220 on the initiative of one of the greatest medieval archbishops, Walter de Grey (1216–55). However, the realization of his conception took two hundred and fifty years, and as late as 1328 the marriage of Edward III and his queen, Philippa of Hainault, took place in the Norman choir which had not yet been replaced.

The cathedral we see today, although two and a half centuries in the building, has a remarkable harmony. It spans all the phases of English Gothic, from Early English through Decorated to Perpendicular. The first parts to be built were the north and south transepts. With their soaring piers, clustered

The great east window, the largest area of painted medieval glass anywhere and ranking in

quality with Chartres. It is supported by a beautiful internal screen of open stonework.

rounded shafts, and columns of Purbeck marble, they set the scale for what was to follow, a building of enormous size and almost overwhelming spaciousness. At the end of the thirteenth century York acquired its chapter-house, one of the finest examples of the early Decorated style. This has no central column, for its vault is of wood, but all around are marvellous and intricately carved canopy stalls. The nave and the north-west front,

Incised columns in the crypt, which is all that remains of the Norman cathedral.

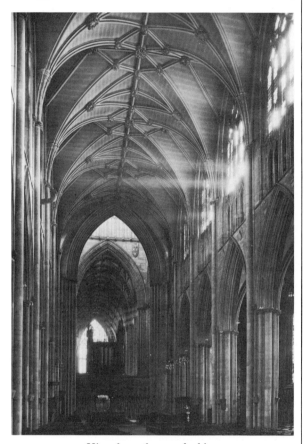

View down the nave looking east towards the choir.

with its magnificent window, were built during the first half of the fourteenth century, followed at the end of that century by the choir, a supreme exercise in the Perpendicular style with walls of glass. The central tower collapsed in a storm in 1407 and the present central tower dates from twenty years after that. The south-west and north-west towers were then added, and with their completion and the installation of the superb pulpitum with its carved ranks of English kings the minster was complete.

Throughout the Middle Ages city and minster played a prominent part in English history. William of Hatfield, infant son of Edward III, was buried here. During his troubled reign King Richard II paid several visits to the city, and after his deposition and murder one of the prebendaries, who resembled him, sought to impersonate the dead king and head a revolt.

In 1405 there was another rebellion, this time headed by Archbishop Scrope. He was condemned in his own palace of Bishopsthorpe and executed, but the fierce independence of Yorkshiremen made his tomb a place of pilgrimage thereafter.

Throughout the fifteenth century York's importance declined, though the city played a key part in the insurrection of 1536 known as the Pilgrimage of Grace, sympathy for which was partly provoked by the way in which the shrine of St William Fitzherbert had been despoiled. After this pilgrimage the minster suffered further plunder but surprisingly little damage was done to York's glass. The cathedral's greatest glory, it also survived the Civil War when the Yorkshireman Lord Fairfax, the Parliamentary general who directed the siege of York, insisted that the minster should be preserved.

York's major disasters occurred during the early nineteenth century: two fires in 1829 and 1840, the first caused by a mad arsonist and the second by a workman's candle. Between them they destroyed much of the medieval woodwork, including the choir stalls. But the greatest danger to the minster arose in the present century, when (in 1967) it was discovered that the central tower was in imminent danger of collapse. An appeal for two million pounds was launched and during the course of a massive five-year restoration programme supervised by Bernard Feilden, an architect of extraordinary ability, new foundations of steel and concrete were inserted and the cathedral was cleaned both inside and out.

With the cleaning the two most notable features of York could at last be fully appreciated, the wonderful sense of spaciousness and the marvellous collection of medieval glass, the largest in this country, and almost of a quality to rival the finest glass of France. The sense of space and height can best be appreciated by standing under the central tower and looking up, or by going to the west door and looking down the full length of the nave towards the east before walking the length of it and looking back. Both east and west windows are of enormous size and great beauty. The west window, given by Archbishop William Melton in 1338, is especially famous. It is known as the 'Heart of York' because the tracery at the top suggests the shape of a heart.

York's stained or, as it is more properly called, painted glass, has been the subject of careful restoration. Here we can see more completely than in any other English cathedral how the stories of the Bible and the saints were told to an unlettered people in the Middle Ages. In one window, for instance, we have the story of St Cuthbert, in another a splendidly graphic illustration of the Stem of Jesse, with a glittering assembly of the medieval artists' conceptions of the chief Old Testament figures. One of York's most famous windows has no figures in it at all. It consists of five soaring fifty-foot-high lancets known as the Five Sisters. Dating from the middle of the thirteenth century, it is the best example in England of that gently coloured glass known as grisaille.

The only way to study and understand York's windows is to spend a couple of hours with a pair of binoculars. You must allow more time than that here, however, for there are other great treasures too. The statues on the choir screen of the kings of England from William the Conqueror to Henry VI are all, save the last, contemporary with the screen's late fifteenth-century construction. The ceiling of the chapter-house has been marvellously restored. The high altar by William Tapper and the font by Ninian Comper are both worthy twentieth-century additions to the minster, and though we must lament the destruction of 1829, the nineteenth-century stalls which replaced the medieval ones do not disgrace the choir.

Of the tombs the most fascinating are the three seventeenth-century ones by Grinling Gibbons, whose work at St Paul's is entirely worthy of Wren's great masterpiece.

York's most recent treasure is an astronomical clock, placed here in 1955 as a memorial to the airmen of Britain and its allies who died operating from bases in the north-east during the Second World War. But it is in the crypt, part of which survives from the Norman cathedral, that we can see both the oldest parts of York and the newest, for here are those reassuringly massive new foundations which ensure that the mother church of the north of England can survive another thousand years.

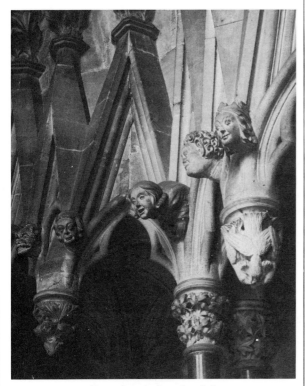

*Carved capitals and corbels
in the chapter-house.*

HENRY VIII'S CATHEDRALS

BRISTOL

The Cathedral Church of the Holy and Undivided Trinity

It is not often that a cathedral suffers by comparison with a parish church but, because many authorities on English churches have echoed Elizabeth I's comment that St Mary Redcliffe was the finest church in her kingdom, today many who go to Bristol to see St Mary's seem unaware that the cathedral is, if not in the very first rank of cathedrals, nevertheless a remarkably fine and distinguished one.

Though its exterior is, on close inspection, undistinguished, it is suitably imposing when seen across College Green, especially when floodlit, and positively breathtaking inside. Go and see, and you may well find yourself agreeing with Nikolaus Pevsner that the early thirteenth-century work here is 'from the point of view of spatial imagination . . . superior to anything else built in England, and indeed in Europe at the same time'.

Bristol was one of those great churches which were given cathedral status by Henry VIII in 1542, at the same time as Gloucester, Chester, Peterborough and Westminster. Since then, save for the period between 1836 and 1897, it has been a full cathedral, the centre of one of the more important dioceses. Indeed, for the long period when Bristol ranked as the second port and city of the realm its cathedral had a special importance.

The floodlit cathedral seen across College Green –
the best vantage point.

Looking down the nave – completed, after four hundred years, in the nineteenth century by G. E. Street.

The Norman chapter-house, still a remarkable example of Romanesque work in spite of the damage caused during the Reform riots of 1831.

It was founded as the church of the Augustinian abbey by Robert Fitzharding, first Lord Berkeley, in 1140. Church and abbey were consecrated about thirty years later, but nothing survives of these Norman buildings except the lower part of the abbey gatehouse, the arches into the cloisters, the undercroft of the refectory, traces of the walls in the south transept and, most important of all, the Norman chapter-house. One of the finest Norman rooms in England, it was damaged during the riots which erupted at the time of the first Reform Bill in 1831 but was sensitively restored and, but for the east wall, still remains much as it was in Fitz-Harding's day. Rib-vaulted and richly ornamented with zigzags and lozenges, and with a marvellous blank arcade of intersected arches, it is a rare treasure indeed.

Early in the thirteenth-century Abbot David built a Lady Chapel, now known as the Elder Lady Chapel. He wrote to the Dean of Wells asking him to send carvers to adorn his chapel, and there are many similarities between the carving here and the famous capitals at Wells.

However, what gives Bristol its real importance is the work of Abbot Knowle, begun in August 1298 and continued almost until his death in 1332. He created what is in fact the only hall church in England. Common in Germany, these are the great churches in which the roofs of nave and aisles all reach to the same height, without any triforium or clerestory. And so Knowle's Lady Chapel is the same height as choir and ambulatory, and its vault, the first lierne vault in England, continues the whole length of the choir. The fifty-foot-high arches are the tallest in England. The whole magnificent effect is of great space enclosed with a beauty and a harmony not quite matched anywhere else. It proves, says Pevsner, 'that English design surpassed that of all other countries during the first third of the fourteenth century'. Mercifully it has been sensitively restored and not altered.

Little was done at Bristol after the death of Abbot Knowle until the last quarter of the fifteenth century, when the south transept was completed and the north transept and crossing and tower were built. Abbot Newland, who died in 1515, began work on the nave which reached the sill height of the outer windows, but Bristol had to wait for its nave and west towers for another three hundred and fifty years! The last major pre-Reformation addition was the fine reredos installed by Abbot Burton (1526–39).

The south choir aisle of England's only great hall church, with the tallest arches and first lierne vaulting in England.

Rededicated to the Holy and Undivided Trinity, the church became Bristol's cathedral in 1552 when a dean and canons replaced the abbot and his Augustinian canons. There is an interesting sidelight on the history of the first bishop, Paul Bush from Edington in Wiltshire. He was forced to retire in 1553 by the devoutly Roman Catholic Mary Tudor because he had married. Today he lies gaunt and without vestments, in one of Bristol's more interesting tombs.

To adorn and beautify the new cathedral the screen was bought from the Carmelite church at Bristol, the gift of a prosperous city merchant, but the statues, or 'images' as the reformers called them, were casualties of Puritan zeal, and the organ which was originally placed on it was destroyed during the troubles of the seventeenth century. However, it is still a notable feature of the cathedral, as is the late seventeenth-century organ case that now adorns it.

The prosperity enjoyed by Bristol in the seventeenth century is reflected in some of the cathedral's furnishings, and especially in its silver plate. The candlesticks which stand on the altar of the eastern Lady Chapel are particularly beautiful. They were a gift from a town clerk who had a great interest in the expedition which captured a Spanish treasure galleon and incidentally rescued Alexander Selkirk, the original Robinson Crusoe, from Juan Fernandez Island.

Though Bristol had one very great bishop in the eighteenth century, Bishop Butler, the story of the cathedral during that century is like that of most others. It was a period of indolence and decay.

After the devastation of the Reform riots of 1831 came demotion. From 1836 to 1897 there was no bishop here for the see was united with that of Gloucester, and it is rather paradoxical that the building of the nave and tower occurred during that period. It can be said of Bristol therefore that almost nothing of importance was built while it actually enjoyed the status of a cathedral. G. E. Street was responsible for the nave and he tried to create a Gothic structure that would be in harmony with the glories of Abbot Knowle and Abbot Newland. He lacked the inspiration and genius of his forebears but Pevsner is right to call his work 'the respectable performance of a sensible architect'. The work was in fact completed after Street's death in 1888. After the church had been re-elevated to cathedral status in 1897 Pearson, architect of Truro Cathedral, was employed to supervise a restoration which would make the interior suitable once more for cathedral services and ceremonies.

There are marvellous individual treasures here too. The earliest is a Saxon stone, probably a coffin lid, with a very well preserved carving of the Harrowing of Hell. In the Berkeley Chapel, one of the most beautiful parts of the cathedral, is the oldest brass candelabrum in the country. In the chancel aisle there is a window which is said to have been given by Nell Gwyn as a thanks offering when she recovered from an illness in 1683, and a window almost three centuries older in the Lady Chapel depicts the martyrdom of King Edmund. And there are a number of good tombs and effigies. The best of all is the monument to Maurice, ninth Earl of Berkeley, who was captured by the French at Poitiers in 1356. Ransomed for £2000, he died in 1368.

Bristol is rarely mentioned among the great cathedrals of England, but in spite of the fact that it remained uncompleted for so many centuries its magnificent Norman chapter-house and superb Early English work certainly merit a special journey, and there is no more accessible city in the kingdom.

The Saxon Stone – a coffin lid found under the chapter-house floor in 1831. It shows the Harrowing of Hell and is one of England's finest Saxon carvings.

CHESTER

Cathedral Church of Christ and the Blessed Virgin Mary

I first visited Chester towards the end of the 1960s. I was excited by the city – I browsed along The Rows, walked the walls, and saved the visit to the cathedral until last. My first impression was one of bitter disappointment. There was nothing to excite me outside. Inside the restorers had obviously had a field day. It was a dull afternoon and it was certainly not brightened by the bad Victorian glass. But I had come to Evensong and that meant seeing the choir stalls. I had heard they were good. They were so outstandingly, excitingly beautiful that I stayed and lingered when the choristers had gone and learned, not for the first time, never to dismiss a building merely because my initial reaction was one of disappointment.

No one could pretend that Chester is among England's greatest cathedrals, but it has many redeeming features, including one of surpassing beauty, and it is set in the midst of the best-preserved group of monastic buildings in the country. Anyone who has wandered through the ruins of Fountains or Rievaulx Abbey and wondered how a complete medieval abbey would have looked should

A carving in the choir stalls, which are perhaps the finest example of late fourteenth-century wood-carving in northern Europe.

come here. Then there would be no need of artist's reconstructions to demonstrate what such a building was like before Henry VIII indulged in the most systematic act of vandalism in English history.

A church was built on this site early in the tenth century to house the already hallowed bones of the Saxon Saint Werburgh, the daughter of Wulfhere, King of Mercia. The only remains of that Saxon church are the traces of two doorways in the cloister. The history of the great abbey of Chester really begins at the end of the eleventh century, when Saint Anselm (soon to become Archbishop of Canterbury) was here. He refounded the abbey as a house of the Benedictine Order and staffed it with monks from his former abbey of Bec in Normandy. This building was briefly the cathedral for Mercia between 1075 and 1095, and we can see marked out on the floor of the present cathedral the places occupied by the apses of the choir and aisle in the Norman church, and of two arches in what is now the baptistry in the north transept.

Between the middle of the thirteenth and the middle of the sixteenth centuries a new abbey church was built, a curiously lop-sided building with the south transept much bigger than the north one, where the presence of the other monastic buildings precluded extension. It was a dual-purpose church. Here the monks said their daily offices and here, until the middle of the fourteenth century, the south aisle acted as the parish church of the garrison town of Chester. After the nave had been rebuilt the townsfolk were given another parish church within the cathedral, this time in the south transept, an arrangement which persisted until 1881. Unlike the great abbeys that were set in the midst of open and often desolate country, Chester had a close association with the town. It was here, for instance, that the celebrated cycle of mystery plays, recently revived, was first performed in the fourteenth century.

In 1540 the abbey was forced to surrender its land and buildings to Henry VIII and then, in July 1541, the former abbey of Saint Werburgh became the Cathedral Church of Christ and the Blessed Virgin Mary to serve the new Chester diocese. There followed a long period of relative obscurity. One

*A general view of the choir stalls with
their graceful, elegant canopies.*

local historian commented that at the time of the refoundation Chester Cathedral from the south presented a sight 'but little inferior in real beauty to any one in England – Canterbury, York and Salisbury excepted'. We will never know how far his judgement was influenced by familiarity. So much damage was done during the seventeenth century to the canopies and traceries of the windows, for instance, that the prospect he praised was destroyed. The Civil War brought great destruction

here for Chester was an important Royalist centre – an allegiance it was not allowed to forget during the Commonwealth.

After the restoration of the monarchy Bishop Nicholas Stratford began a programme of repair but his successors did not emulate him. By 1818 the cathedral Chapter Book was recording that the building had 'from long neglect fallen in many parts into great decay'. Unfortunately much of the earlier restoration was done with little sympathy for the

*The somewhat unimposing
exterior of Chester
cathedral.*

medieval character of the church. Chester's major restoration dates from 1868 and was begun by George Gilbert Scott. He was followed by the Blomfields, father and son, and their work amounted almost to a rebuilding, creating a Victorian church within the shell of a medieval one.

Mercifully the restorers did nothing to damage or detract from the beauty of Chester's superb choir stalls. Dating from the last two decades of the fourteenth century, they are without question the finest in England. The forty-eight misericords are exquisitely carved and between them show a pageant of medieval life and fable, together with some marvellous representations of biblical scenes such as the magnificent misericord of Easter morning. The visitor to Chester should certainly come armed with a torch and take time to admire these rare masterpieces. The misericords, however, are not the only great wood carvings here. The canopies over the stalls are again the finest examples of their kind, and there is a superb figure of a pilgrim at the end of what was the abbot's, and is now the dean's, stall. In the history of English art, Chester's choir stalls are as important as the Leaves of Southwell.

There are other things too which deserve attention, including the only surviving old consistory court in England. The bishop's special court, it has furnishings given by Charles I's Bishop of Chester, John Bridgeman, who also gave the screen which separates the court from the nave.

It is important to take the time to see just what the Victorians did during those last thirty years of the nineteenth century, when the whole appearance of the cathedral was completely altered. The old stone pulpitum went and was replaced by a wooden one. A mosaic by Salviati was installed behind the high altar. Encaustic tiles were put down in the choir and sanctuary and new windows were inserted, mostly filled with indifferent glass, although there is one interesting Resurrection by Pugin. It is impossible not to regret what has gone, but the quality of much of the Victorian craftsmanship and carving is such that the craftsmen deserve praise even if the architects merit rebuke. The most fascinating set of nineteenth-century corbels is here, for instance. They are delightful caricatures of Gladstone and Disraeli.

Apart from the choir, Chester's most interesting work is not in the main cathedral at all but in the remarkably fine collection of monastic buildings around. Here is the only early thirteenth-century chapter-house with a fine set of lancet windows to have survived almost intact. More important even than that is the abbey refectory with its stone pulpit built into the wall, where a monk would read to the brethren at meals.

The cloisters have been brought back into use and Chester has one very modern addition, too, a free-

*One of the forty-eight magnificent
misericords in the
choir stalls.*

standing bell tower designed by George Pace and opened in 1975. From here the bells which used to hang in the cathedral's centre tower regularly ring out over Chester. Would that everybody responsible for twentieth-century additions to medieval buildings had had the tact and sensitivity of the Dean and Chapter of Chester, who placed their modern tower, a pleasing enough work in its own right, fifty yards away from the cathedral building. It is just a pity that their Victorian predecessors were not similarly careful.

GLOUCESTER

The Cathedral Church of the Holy Trinity

No cathedral city has been less sympathetically developed in the present century than Gloucester – even much of the close itself has been turned into a vast car park. Nothing, however, can detract from the glorious symmetry of the cathedral tower, nor from the combination of massive grandeur and ethereal grace within. Nor has any cathedral had greater good fortune in the choice of its recent deans than Gloucester. Too often one gets the impression that twentieth-century clerics regard the great buildings and precious objects committed to their charge as encumbrances. Seiriol Evans and Gilbert Thurlow really knew the meaning of worshipping the Lord in the beauty of holiness and Gloucester is the better for their stewardship.

Gloucester is another of the great Benedictine abbey churches saved from dereliction by Henry VIII. He nominated this as the cathedral church for a new diocese carved out of the ancient see of Worcester. It owed its salvation and its great eminence and beauty largely to the fact that it was a church rich in royal associations. In the charter Henry VIII issued when he founded the see he proclaimed that 'considering the site of the said late monastery in which many famous monuments of our renowned ancestors, Kings of England, are erected, is a very fit and

The great east window, known as the Crécy window. It is the largest in England – 34 feet wide and 72 feet high.

proper place . . . we have decreed that the site of the said monastery be an episcopal see . . . and we also will and ordain that the said Dean and Prebendaries, and their successors shall forever hereafter be called the Dean and Chapter of the Holy and Undivided Trinity of Gloucester.'

There was a monastery founded here by Osric, Prince of Mercia, as early as 681, and though the foundation had a far from tranquil history, the church and monastic buildings being twice destroyed, such was Gloucester's strategic importance as one of the main cities of Saxon England that it was refounded, first in 823 and then, as a Benedictine house, in 1048. Edward the Confessor stayed here and held a council in the monastery, and before that King Alfred's saintly daughter Ethelfleda was buried in the abbey church of St Peter.

The majestic Norman nave with its cylindrical piers – very similar to those in the other great Gloucestershire Benedictine abbey of Tewkesbury.

The elegant and superbly beautiful fifteenth-century tower.

Important in Saxon times, Gloucester's strategic position was not lost on William the Conqueror, and though by 1066 the monastery was almost at the point of extinction, with only two monks and eight novices in residence, the Conqueror was determined that it should be maintained. He appointed his chaplain Serlo, from Mont Saint Michel, as abbot and by the time of his death in 1104 one hundred monks were in residence. A great new abbey church was dedicated on 15 July 1100, the last year of the reign of William Rufus, by Sampson, Bishop of Worcester, Gundulph, Bishop of Rochester, and Harvey, Bishop of Bangor.

Of the church Serlo built, only the crypt remains and that was strengthened and added to in later years to bear the weight of the building above. In the twelfth century Gloucester became one of the greatest of Benedictine houses and it is from this period that much of the nave dates, with its magnificent and massive pillars and round arches. Some idea of the importance of the church is given by the presence of the finest of the few early wooden effigies

in existence, for before the high altar we can see a thirteenth-century representation of Robert Curthose, eldest son of the Conqueror and his successor as Duke of Normandy. He died in captivity in Cardiff Castle in 1134, having been captured at Tinchbrai twenty-eight years previously by Henry I. Curthose was a weak and treacherous man but he was William's eldest son, and that he should have been brought and laid to rest here says something for the high regard in which the abbey church of Gloucester was held at the time.

Before his burial the church had been swept by fire, as were so many of the wooden-roofed churches of Saxon and Norman England. The Anglo-Saxon Chronicle tells us that in 1122, as the monks were singing Mass, a mighty fire burst from the upper part of the steeple and burnt the whole of the monastery. Nearly seventy years later, in 1190, another fire destroyed most of the city and many of the buildings of the monastery. Between 1242 and 1245 the nave was given a new stone vault and immediately afterwards a south-west tower, later destroyed, was built. The stone vaulting was, we are told, erected by the monks themselves and, though it was a tribute to their devotion, its proportions do much to spoil the great beauty of the nave.

In 1216 another great royal event took place here when Henry III, a boy of only nine, was crowned on 28 October, following the sudden death of King John at Newark. The story is that he was crowned with his mother's bracelet and there is a Victorian window in the south aisle of the nave to commemorate the event.

The fourteenth century was the great age of building in Gloucester. In 1327 Edward II was murdered at nearby Berkeley Castle at the instigation of his wife Isabella and her lover, Roger, Earl Mortimer. Abbot John Thoky moved the body here from Berkeley in his own chariot, and Edward was buried amid scenes of great solemnity in the presence of his widow and of the young King Edward III, who ordered that a suitably magnificent monument be created to his father. The king who had been despised for his weakness and sodomy during his life was now venerated as a martyr. Within a few years his tomb was regarded as a shrine and Gloucester became a great pilgrim centre. Wherever there were pilgrims in the Middle Ages there was money to be made, and it was from their offerings that the burial place of Edward II became the birthplace of that glorious and particularly English adaptation of the Gothic which we know today as Perpendicular architecture.

Thus it is that today we pass from the great round columns of the nave into a miraculously beautiful choir. This is one of the great romances of medieval architecture. From engravings of Old St Pauls, the great London cathedral which perished in the fire of 1666, it would seem that it had many affinities with what now exists at Gloucester. Here we can see soaring columns, a great lierne vault ninety-two feet above the floor, and the largest stained glass window in England, still – in spite of the damage of six centuries – full of wonderful fourteenth-century glass. Very probably the gift of Lord Bradstone, whose arms it shows, it is known as the Crécy window as both he and his friend Sir Maurice Berkeley, also commemorated, fought there in 1346. The window shows the coronation of the Virgin, the twelve apostles surrounded by saints, and, in the lowest tier, abbots of Gloucester and bishops of Worcester. Together with the flying arches and the orchestra of angelic musicians forming the bosses in the vault above the high altar, the whole composition, as Alec Clifton Taylor says, 'leaves one gasping with admiration at its brilliant audacity'.

Whilst all this exuberant creative activity was

Fan vaulting in the cloisters, the first and the most extensive in England.
On the left are recesses in which the monks worked at wooden desks.

An orchestra of angelic musicians in the roof above the choir – an early example of lierne vaulting.

going on, Richard II came here in 1378 and held a parliament in the monastery buildings.

After the choir was completed and the north transept remodelled, work began on the cloisters. Finished around 1420 they are the most splendid and extensive cloisters in England, with the first significant fan vaulting in the country. No one should visit Gloucester without allowing plenty of time to see them. Here, more than anywhere, we can get an idea of how the monks passed their time. We can see the row of twenty recesses, or carrels, where each would study at a wooden desk, and the remarkable lavatorium, the long lead-lined water trough where they washed.

Work continued on extending and enriching the great abbey church throughout the fifteenth century. The west front was added between 1450 and 1460, and in the time of Abbot Seabroke the central tower was built; it is one of the most beautifully and delicately proportioned in the whole of Europe. Then came the final adornment, the Lady Chapel. Finished at the very end of the fifteenth century, it is the consummation of the Perpendicular style, with its wonderfully vaulted roof and walls of light. Perhaps its most distinguishing and elegant feature is the bridge which links the north and south triforia across the chapel and which has the properties of a whispering gallery.

This then was the abbey church which surrendered to the king in 1540 and, along with all the other buildings of the great Benedictine house, was then transformed from St Peters into the Cathedral of the Holy and Undivided Trinity. Probably because of its royal associations and monuments, it suffered less than most great churches at the hands of the zealots who destroyed in the name of 'the primitive and genuine rule of simplicity'. There was no shrine here to despoil.

Gloucester suffered little too during the Civil War, but much of its ancient glass was smashed and at one stage work actually began on the demolition of the Lady Chapel. And it escaped lightly in the eighteenth and nineteenth centuries though the medieval pulpitum was destroyed and replaced, in 1820, by the present choir screen. As a guide book written in 1897 says, 'Gloucester has suffered somewhat at the hands of Sir Gilbert Scott, but probably not a tithe of what would have been inflicted upon it had Wyatt been turned loose with an absolutely free hand'.

The angels of the choir vault and the figures in the great Crécy window are among the most memorable of all Gloucester's treasures, but this is a cathedral full of interesting things, ranging from the sixteenth-century cope chest and a memorial to Jenner, discoverer of smallpox vaccination, to the simple stone cross carved by Colonel Carne of the Gloucesters during his imprisonment in the Korean war in 1951. Undoubtedly the most beautiful monuments are those to Robert Curthose and to Edward II, which is the finest alabaster figure of the fourteenth century. Among other features are a series of misericords and, in the south transept, the so-called 'Prentice Bracket' in the form of a mason's set square. It shows a young man falling, and is reckoned to commemorate an apprentice who fell to his death while working on the vault above. There are good things from the nineteenth century here too, including Scott's reredos behind the high altar.

The chapter-house, part of the Norman abbey and extended in the fifteenth century, was further restored in 1981 and its accoustics improved as a memorial of the thirteenth centenary of the foundation. It is now used as a conference centre. It was here that William I had one of his most significant conferences when, in conclave with his barons at Christmas 1085, he gave the order for the compilation of the Domesday Book, that remarkable inventory of eleventh-century England.

The tomb of Edward II, perhaps the finest of all medieval royal effigies. Edward was buried here after his murder at nearby Berkeley Castle.

OXFORD

The Cathedral Church of Christ the King

Oxford is the most unusual of all England's cathedrals. Very much the smallest of them, it has a history quite unlike that of any other, and surroundings which effectively disguise its identity for many visitors. The first time I came here as a schoolboy I did not know that I had been to a cathedral until afterwards, and many visitors today who come and admire the college chapel of Christ Church do not realize that they are also admiring the cathedral of the diocese of Oxford. It is in fact the only cathedral in the world which serves as a college chapel, or perhaps it would be more accurate to say that this is the only college chapel in the world that serves as a cathedral.

The first church on this site was a Saxon nunnery which was allegedly founded by another of that seeming multitude of saintly Saxon ladies of royal lineage, Frideswide. Here in the seventh century, having repudiated the advances of a princely lover, Frideswide, we are told, persuaded her father to found her a nunnery where she could preside over twelve virgins of noble birth. The persistent prince was struck blind when he made further advances, and then healed by the saintly princess, whose remains, when she died, were enshrined in the nunnery she had established.

It is always difficult to separate truth from legend

Civil War monuments in the north aisle of the choir recall the days when Charles I held his court here during the Great Rebellion.

with any degree of precision but we do know that early in the twelfth century, having been alternatively nunnery and monastery, St Frideswide's became an Augustinian priory. So it remained, a centre of no particularly notable intellectual vigour or great piety, throughout the thirteenth and fourteenth centuries. The shrine of its founder made it a place of pilgrimage but, though the emerging university was attracting scholars to Oxford, St Fridiswide's seems to have been unfortunate in its priors, and there are numerous accounts of their getting into debt and being much involved in the early 'town versus gown' riots.

In the fifteenth century the priory obtained a new dignity when the Pope granted its prior the right to wear a mitre. In 1524, however, the priory of St Frideswide was dissolved by another Pope on the petition of Cardinal Wolsey who wanted to create a great college at Oxford and to incorporate the former priory church in his scheme of things. To be called Cardinal College, it was to be the biggest and grandest of all Oxford's colleges, but in 1529 Wolsey fell from favour and the new college passed to the King, who in 1532 refounded it. Ten years later Henry created a diocese of Oxford with the recently suppressed abbey at nearby Oseney as its centre. It made little sense, however, for the centre of the diocese to be away from the increasingly important university city, and so in 1546 the new

The early thirteenth-century spire of Christ Church seen from Corpus Christi. It is among the oldest stone spires in England.

*The nave looking east towards the point where the Norman gives way to the pendent
lierne vaulting of the Tudor choir.*

bishopric of Oxford was refounded and the college chapel became the cathedral church of Christ the King. Though it had its origins in Henry's desire to appropriate as many revenues as possible and to economize by combining college and cathedral, no subsequent king or bishop has made any attempt to alter the situation and so college chapel and cathedral have remained as one to this day.

The new cathedral inevitably suffered during the triumph of the iconoclasts when the shrine of St Frideswide was destroyed. Her bones were buried secretly. Some years later the wife of one of the canons, Peter Martyr, died. She had been a nun renowned for her piety and her kindness to the poor, but her marriage was enough to damn her in the eyes of the Roman Catholic hierarchy who returned briefly to power during the short and bitter reign of Mary Tudor, and so she was disinterred. In 1561, with Elizabeth safely on the throne, it was decided to give her another decent Christian burial. John Carthill, the sub-dean, who was responsible for arranging this found 'some dark coloured bones' carefully covered up and undamaged in two silken

Samuel, David, John and Timothy,
a pre-Raphaelite window designed
by Burne-Jones.

bags. Deciding that these were the remains of St Frideswide, and to prevent any future violation of the peace of the dead, he put the bones of both holy women together and buried them in a secret place.

Queen Elizabeth, more anxious to receive the revenues from the see than to appoint a Bishop of Oxford, kept the see vacant for thirty years of her long reign (1558–1603). In 1567 she did appoint Hugh Curwen, the Archbishop of Dublin, to the see because he wanted to end his days in Oxford. But he was 'very decrepit with old age and many state affairs' and died the next year. It was twenty-one years before Elizabeth appointed a successor.

Bishop Skinner, who held the see from 1641 to 1663, was put in the Tower for a time by Cromwell because he was vociferous in supporting the rights of the bishops to sit in Parliament. A brave man, he conducted a secret ordination of some three hundred priests during the Commonwealth, and was suitably honoured at the Restoration in 1660 when he was asked to officiate at a mass ordination in Westminster Abbey. It was said of him that he 'sent more labourers into the vineyard than all the brethren he had left behind him had done'.

Among the bishops of the next two centuries undoubtedly the best-known were John Fell (1676–86) and Samuel Wilberforce, son of William, who was bishop from 1845 to 1870, although the most famous nineteenth-century character connected with Christ Church was a little girl, the daughter of Dean Liddell and the inspiration for *Alice's Adventures in Wonderland*.

The cathedral is so small because when Wolsey laid out the great quadrangle (now known as 'Tom Quad') for his college he demolished four of the eight bays of its Norman nave. However, what remains is enough to make this an architecturally interesting, and indeed a distinguished, church. Its instantly recognizable stumpy stone spire, built around 1230, is one of the oldest in the country, and the oldest of all cathedral spires. The massive Norman columns, which date from the beginning of the Augustinian priory at the end of the twelfth century, are especially notable. With their beautifully carved Corinthian capitals, which alone would make them outstanding, they are architecturally unusual as well for they rise above the triforium. Even more remarkable and spectacular, however, is the roof of the choir. This dates from the very first years of the fifteenth century and is held by many to be the best example of its period in any English

*The Becket window. It was preserved by replacing the saint's head with a piece
of plain glass when all effigies of Thomas were being destroyed.*

cathedral. It is a beautiful lierne vault with a difference, for suspended from it are lantern-like pendants. The whole intricate construction is of enormous interest and beauty, a light and airy architectural fantasy which blends surprisingly well with the Norman columns, like cobwebs in a forest.

The cathedral's other notable feature is its fine glass. St Lucy's Chapel, off the south transept, boasts the greatest treasure of all: the Becket window. Dating from the middle of the fourteenth century it commemorates the assassination of Thomas à Becket at Canterbury Cathedral two hundred years before. It owes its preservation to an ingenious cleric who, when Henry VIII ordered that all effigies of Becket should be destroyed, saved the window by removing Becket's face from the glass and substituting a piece of plain glass in its place.

There are rather smaller fragments of fourteenth-century glass in the Latin Chapel, so called because until 1648, and again from the Restoration until 1861, the daily services were said here in Latin. The rest of the glass in the cathedral is mostly of nineteenth-century date but does include fine work by Burne-Jones, William Morris and the firm of Clayton and Bell. Among the other treasures are the fine stalls in the Latin Chapel; the rare wooden watching chamber (one of only two in existence) where visitors to the shrine could be observed; the Jacobean pulpit; and a splendid series of Cavalier monuments to those who lost their lives fighting for the King in the Civil War, when the Royalist capital was at Oxford and the King lodged in Christ Church.

Christ Church also has some magnificent plate and a very beautiful Early English chapter-house with painted roundels of the thirteenth century and beautiful roof bosses. There is some more good glass here and – an interesting reminder of the founder of the college the cathedral serves – the foundation stone of the grammar school that Wolsey founded in his own town of Ipswich in 1528, just before his fall.

PETERBOROUGH

The Cathedral Church of St Peter, St Paul and St Andrew

Peterborough is probably the least known of great English cathedrals. Unlike the other cathedrals of the flat lands of eastern England it does not dominate the countryside. Lincoln rises out of the plain, Ely's tower is a true lantern to the Fens, Norwich's spire soars high into the Norfolk sky, but Peterborough stands firm, low and solid, an almost hidden gem. Many of those who visit it for the first time will, however, have a feeling of familiarity, for this was the cathedral chosen as Barchester for the television serial based on Trollope's first two Barchester novels.

My most enduring memories of Peterborough will always be of my visit in 1983 when I saw it in circumstances of rare perfection. It was a wet and windy East Anglian afternoon, but inside the cathedral an orchestra was rehearsing Mendelssohn's Violin Concerto and Tchaikovsky's *Symphonie Pathétique*. I had a special, unhurried opportunity to appreciate Peterborough's many beauties, such as the extraordinary painted roof of the nave, and the remarkable series of Benedictine memorials, long lost medieval abbots eternally resting in tonsured tranquillity. Perhaps some of them watched from the small turret in the Chapel of St Oswald over the relic of the martyred King's arm, brought here in the eleventh century. For the first time I was able to enjoy a modern treasure, a lovely Annunciation in the chapel dedicated to two other early English saints, Kyneburga and Kyneswitha, daughters of

Fan vaulting in the retrochoir – magnificent late fourteenth-century work.

Looking upwards beneath the central tower to the vault restored in 1884.

Penda, King of Mercia. It is the work of Alan Durst who was responsible for many of the replacement statues on the west front, and it was placed here as a memorial to his wife. Another touching memorial is the bright window commemorating Canon Twells who dedicated his life to the music of the church, a real-life version of Trollope's Septimus Harding. Memorials like these provide a remarkable thread of continuity in the history of any great church. Peterborough is no exception. Here we see the effigy of the abbot regarded as 'very mild and peaceable' who 'made it his endeavour to plant and establish tranquillity in his flock', qualities also extolled in the grand eighteenth-century tomb of one Thomas

*The striking west front
of Peterborough.*

Deacon whose piety 'consisted not in empty profession but in sincerity and unaffected truth'.

Peterborough became the cathedral of one of the new post-Reformation sees in 1541, but well into the nineteenth century, until the coming of the railway made the town an important thoroughfare, the great church was regarded as the centre of one of the most perfectly preserved examples of a monastic borough. Today even the railway town has been submerged as Peterborough has become the hub of a sprawling new town development. The cathedral, in its close, is an oasis of quiet in an unlovely urban waste-land.

The first monastery established here was founded by the son of King Penda of Mercia in the seventh century. It was destroyed by the Danes some two hundred years later and there is a relic of those troubled times in today's cathedral, the so-called

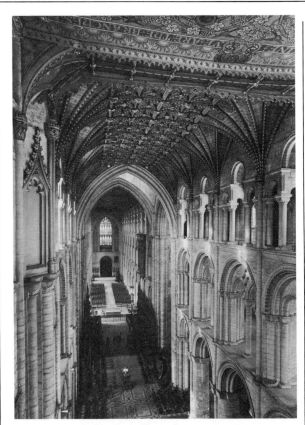

A view from the south-east corner,
showing the magnificence of the Norman work and the
fine painted wooden roof above.

Hedda or Monks' Stone, once thought to be a memorial to the monks slaughtered by the Danes in 870. It is now reckoned to be even older, one of the most priceless relics of Anglo-Saxon sculpture in existence.

In 972 King Edgar directed that a new monastery should be built and this was the sanctuary familiar to Hereward the Wake, the folk hero and Saxon warrior, who held out in the Fenlands against the Normans. It was a place of high importance. Two Archbishops of York were buried there, but in 1116 it was destroyed by a fire which, the old chronicles tell us, raged for nine days. Two years later the foundation of the present great church was laid by Abbot John of Sais.

Throughout the twelfth century they added to the building. At the beginning of the thirteenth century the west front was built and today we see Peterborough much as it was when rededicated by the saintly Robert Grosseteste of Lincoln, in whose diocese it lay, in 1238. There have been additions since, and the central tower has had to be rebuilt

twice, but Peterborough remains one of the least altered of great English Norman churches, only surpassed in importance by Durham.

For three centuries after its rededication it was the centre of one of the most important Benedictine monasteries in the land, but the abbots grew rich and the observance of the rules waned. By the beginning of the sixteenth century it was, like so many of the other monastic houses, much in need of reform.

Peterborough has a particularly poignant link with the Reformation for here in 1536 Catherine of Aragon, Henry's first wife, over whose divorce the political breach with Rome had come, was buried, brought hither in great state after her death at Kimbolton in Huntingdonshire. Her funeral was the last great event in the history of the monastery. Three years later it surrendered its lands into the King's own hands and the church was reconstituted as a cathedral, the last abbot, John Chambers, becoming the first bishop.

As the burial of one queen came at the end of an era so that of another came at the beginning of a new age, for in 1587 the body of Mary Queen of Scots was brought here after her execution at Fotheringhay, and another majestic and solemn ceremony was held as a second sad queen was laid to rest.

In 1621 Mary was reinterred in Westminster Abbey by her son, now James I of England, and during the Civil War the tomb of Catherine of Aragon was smashed and defaced. Today rather garish banners and sombre memorial slabs mark the resting place of these two queens, and one of the first things the visitor sees on entering the church, looking up towards the west window, is a memorial to the man who buried them, a remarkable local character called Roger Scarlett, sexton and grave-digger for most of the sixteenth century. He died in 1594 at the age of ninety-eight after, we are told, having outlived the two queens and two generations of every household in the town.

Catherine of Aragon's tomb was not the only casualty of the Civil War, for almost every major monument was defaced, every window broken, and most brasses pulled up. For two centuries afterwards the cathedral was sadly neglected, but those who restored it in the nineteenth century were more sensitive than many of their colleagues charged with similar duties in other places. Today, in spite of neglect and restoration, many glories remain, the chief of which is the amazing painted roof of the nave. Dating from the second decade of the thirteenth century, it is one of the most important medieval works of art in existence, a fantastic series of saints, kings, bishops, beasts and monsters. It can only be properly appreciated with the aid of binoculars. Position yourself well and stare down into the trolley placed in the nave and you will see the most remarkable series of medieval figure studies in all England.

There is a fine roof in the presbytery dating from the fifteenth century and though the central tower was rebuilt in 1884 its wonderful vaulted ceiling, dominated by the roof boss of Christ in Majesty, has been sensitively restored. The interior of Peterborough is of limestone from nearby Barnack. It is a stone that has stood the test of time well and assists the blending of the Norman, the medieval and the nineteenth-century.

The Norman arches give a feeling of solid dependability. There is something very reassuring and comforting about them. They are a perfect contrast to the marvellous vaulting of the so-called New Building, which dates from the late fifteenth century and is thought to be the work of the architect of

King's College, Cambridge, that supreme achievement of late medieval art.

There are many individual treasures here, such as the three double piscinas marking the sites of altars, an outstanding brass lectern which survived both the Reformation and the Civil War, and a fine nineteenth-century canopy over the altar before the apse. Peterborough also has a notable cathedral treasury, donated by the Worshipful Company of Goldsmiths and opened in 1981 in the former library. Here some of the finest examples of the cathedral's plate, and plate from parishes throughout the diocese, are displayed, and many of the books from the old library are to be seen in the gallery.

Perhaps the most memorable twentieth-century monument is one to another woman who, like Peterborough's queens, had a tragic death: Nurse Cavell, shot for helping Belgian and French soldiers to escape from Belgium in the First World War. She was buried in Norwich but went to school here, and the tablet was erected 'by teachers, pupils and friends of her old school'.

The Hedda stone, thought to be a memorial to the monks slain by the Danes in 870.

ANCIENT FOUNDATIONS: NEW DESIGNATIONS

RIPON

The Cathedral Church of St Peter and St Wilfrid

Ripon's great treasure, appropriately now the home of the cathedral's own treasury, is simple, quiet, solid and very ancient – its Saxon crypt. In truth not much of the crypt is as St Wilfrid would have known it, but enough survives to make us realize that here we are standing at the very foundation of Christianity in northern England. For this is part of the church Wilfrid founded in the middle of the seventh century to be the guardian of the faith in the Saxon kingdom of Northumbria. From here, as Bishop of York, he ruled the diocese of the north, building a church which owed much to what he had seen when he had travelled to Rome.

*The west front
with its two
low towers.*

It is here in the place where the bones and relics of Yorkshire's earliest Christians were once kept that we should begin a visit to one of those great collegiate churches which were elevated to cathedral status in the last century. For Ripon, like Southwell, was one of the three mother churches of the great archdiocese of York, though after Wilfrid's time it lost any claim to cathedral status until 1836 when it became the centre of a new diocese. As at Southwell, the Archbishops of York once had a palace at Ripon and again, as at Southwell, they established a college of secular canons who ministered to the needs of the town and surrounding country.

Wilfrid's Saxon church was laid waste by the Danes and destroyed, save for part of the crypt. The early days after the Conquest were dark too, for Ripon and the surrounding countryside suffered much during William's victorious 'harrying of the north' in 1069, when the second church on the site was destroyed.

Gradually peace came and under Thomas of Bayeux, the first Norman Archbishop of York who loved this place, a new church rose, a church from which Archbishop Thurston and a body of monks went out to found Fountains Abbey just two miles away. Though there are small traces of this Norman building in the undercroft and elsewhere, the church we see today goes back to, and is an extension of, the fourth church on the site, built by Archbishop Roger, who took Henry II's side in that most celebrated of the many quarrels between medieval kings and prelates, Henry's feud with Thomas à Becket. From Archbishop Roger's church the north transept and part of the north side of the choir survive, together with the chapter-house which he converted from the earlier church.

During the first half of the thirteenth century

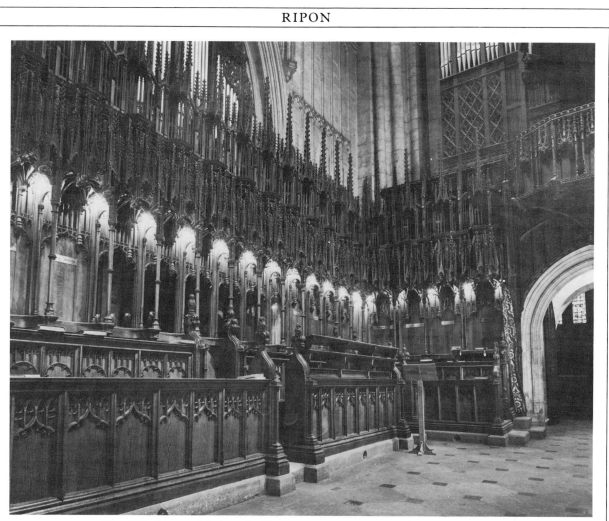

The richly decorated choir stalls. They contain a notable set of thirty-four misericords with some fine animal carving.

Archbishop Walter de Grey supervised yet another rebuilding. He it was who was responsible for the plain but dignified Early English west front with its series of lancet windows and its twin squat towers, which he crowned with wooden spires. Towards the end of the thirteenth century Archbishop Romanus rebuilt the eastern part of the choir, demanding that each canon should contribute a tithe, or tenth, of the income of his prebend until the work was complete. The rest of the money was raised by the sale of indulgences, those medieval documents which served as insurance policies for the wayward in fear of damnation.

Early in the fourteenth century Ripon was plundered by the invading Scots during their period of mastery in the north after the battle of Bannockburn (1314), but peace returned and the shrine of St Wilfrid became one of the major pilgrimage centres of the north. Then in 1450 part of the central tower collapsed and the church was neglected throughout the fifteenth-century civil war we know as the Wars of the Roses, when some of the bloodiest battles ever fought in England took place in Yorkshire, at Wakefield and at Towton, both only forty miles away.

The central tower was never completely rebuilt but in the last decade of the fifteenth century the marvellous choir stalls were erected with their elaborately carved misericords – still very entertaining in spite of heavy restoration in the last century.

During the first half of the sixteenth century the nave was rebuilt and then the College of Canons was, unlike many of the secular colleges, dissolved by Henry VIII. However, it was re-established in 1604 by James I and it is to this re-establishment that we owe the fact that Ripon, alone of the parish church cathedrals, has a dean and not a provost.

Like most cathedrals, Ripon's history is marred by stories of smashing and desecration during the Reformation period and, more particularly, during the Civil War. In 1660 the spire of the central tower fell, causing great damage to the choir stalls, and for safety's sake the spires on the top of the twin towers of the west front were removed in 1664. After a period of eighteenth-century neglect extensive surgical restoration took place in the nineteenth century, much of it after Ripon's elevation to cathedral status in 1836.

In Ripon we have that extraordinary case of a notable feature spoiling a beautiful view, for the fifteenth-century pulpitum with the organ above it completely blocks the vista from west door to east window. The pulpitum itself has been filled with all manner of coloured statues which from a distance look rather as if Madame Tussaud had been let loose here. Ripon's most elegant adornments are undoubtedly the pinnacled canopies above the choir stalls and canons' seats and the restorations there, necessary after the disaster of 1660 and added to in the last century, have fortunately been sensitive.

At the east end is Ninian Comper's notably successful reredos, a memorial to the men of Ripon killed in the 1914–18 war. It helps to set off the magnificent tracery of the east window, filled, alas, with rather inferior nineteenth-century glass. There are good roof bosses above the choir, among them a delightfully prudish one of Adam and Eve; and precious manuscripts, including King James I's

flamboyantly illuminated Charter of Restoration, in the library.

The Chapel of the Holy Spirit in the south choir aisle is separated by a screen created by Leslie Durban in 1970, a mass of oddly twisted metal looking at first sight like rows of bent sword blades and corkscrews, but somehow not jarring.

Among the smaller features I particularly like the misericord of Samson carrying off the gates of Gaza, something he would probably not have been able to do in fifteenth-century Ripon, where the curfew was sounded every night by the Wakeman. It

The south transept from the head of the nave. On the left is the stone pulpitum with its painted figures.

is still sounded today in a tradition that spans the centuries just as this cathedral, with its Saxon crypt, links us with the coming of the faith to the north.

Ripon does not excite. It is one of the smaller and less remarkable cathedrals. But, as with all the major English churches, it is well worth a visit. John Harvey says of its nave, 'it remains one of the most intriguing of our might have beens ... the germ from which sprang another and still more brilliant architecture'.

The Saxon crypt – one of the most hallowed spots in the history of English Christianity.

ST ALBANS

The Cathedral and Abbey Church of St Alban

In AD 209 a Briton living in the Roman city of Verulamium gave refuge to a persecuted Christian priest. He was converted and baptized and when the soldiers came to his house he exchanged cloaks with his guest and was taken before the Roman magistrate. He proclaimed that he believed 'in the Living God', and was taken to a hill outside the city walls and beheaded.

So much we know of Alban, England's first native Christian martyr. Within a few years there was a small church on the site of his execution and about five hundred years later an abbey dedicated to his name and his memory was founded here, probably by Offa, King of Mercia. Of this abbey and of those churches which went before, there is no trace. The long, low, sombre church with its squat central tower which stands on the Hertfordshire hilltop today was mainly the work of St Alban's first Norman abbot, Paul of Caen, a friend of Archbishop Lanfranc.

They had no stones here and so to glorify the Christian saint they built a great church with bricks from the ruins of the deserted pagan city. Eight hundred years later, in 1878, the abbey church was designated the cathedral of the new diocese of St Albans. This was no mere elevation of a parish church, though parish church it was. It was the beginning of a new chapter in the history of the church which until the dissolution of the monasteries was the church of the premier English abbey. It was so designated by Nicholas Breakspear, who was born near by. He is the only Englishman ever to have been Pope and when he went to Rome, as Adrian IV, in 1154, he issued a Papal Bull *Incomprehensibilis* in which he decreed that St Albans should be supreme among English monasteries, its abbot

A thirteenth-century painting of the Crucifixion on one of the nave piers.

St Alban's shrine in the sanctuary. The central carving depicts his beheading at the hands of the Romans for his Christian beliefs.

the senior mitred abbot in Parliament. So things remained until the Reformation.

Though sorely altered by a rich but overpowering benefactor in the nineteenth century, St Albans remains quintessentially a great Norman church. Its nave is longer than any other nave in England save that of Winchester, and although the Early English and Decorated styles are represented here, the

*The cathedral from the south-west
with its squat
central tower.*

For three hundred years the church served a small community in a rural town near London. These were quiet years and inevitably because of the size and age of the church they were years of decline and decay. Although the church was the natural choice for the cathedral of the new diocese of Hertfordshire and Bedfordshire the formation of which was announced in 1877, it was in great need of restoration. Then it was that one of those remarkable Victorian benefactors appeared. Sir Edmund Beckett, created first Baron Grimthorpe, was a generous but overbearing vulgarian. He offered to pay for everything, but he dictated everything. Without a doubt

*A view of the only remaining stone
rood screen in an English
cathedral.*

massive core is eleventh-century Norman, built of Roman bricks covered with plaster.

The abbey was much extended during the early years of the thirteenth century. These extensions were in stone as the abbey was now rich, and so there was no financial problem about transportation. Nevertheless the work in the abbey went in fits and starts. The west end was never fully completed, and when early in the fourteenth century five bays on the south side collapsed there was no immediate attempt to rebuild them. Later in that century a screen was added and in 1484 the present reredos.

In 1539 the abbey of St Alban, mighty as it had been, went the way of all the monasteries and surrendered into the hands of the King. The abbey buildings were knocked down and only the church (sold to the townspeople to be their parish church) and the abbey gatehouse survived.

Inevitably the shrine of St Alban was destroyed, but the wooden watching chamber in which a monk would sit and guard the shrine and watch the pilgrims, a marvellously accomplished piece of fourteenth-century woodwork, is still there.

he saved the church from ruin, but at a price. He was responsible for the west front which is hardly in harmony with the building and he put windows in the transepts without regard for anything save his own taste. One large circular window is known as the Banker's Window for it has apertures corresponding with the sizes of the coins of the realm. Grimthorpe spent lavishly and today the abbey church and cathedral stands secure if mutilated, and still full of treasures. Foremost among these is the amazing series of medieval paintings, which has been restored over the last fifty years. Those on the west side of the pillars portray the Crucifixion in the upper panels, and the Blessed Virgin Mary in the lower. Those on the south represent a number of saints specially popular with pilgrims and including St Christopher, St Thomas of Canterbury and Edward the Confessor. There is an interesting parallel here with Christ Church, Oxford: St Thomas has his face obliterated, just as in the Becket window where it has been replaced with plain glass. Both testify to the passionate hatred of Henry VIII for the saint who had rebuked Henry II.

The pulpitum, though minus its saints, further casualties of Reformation zeal, is a notable fourteenth-century screen and in the presbytery there is a wooden vaulted roof a hundred years older and a fifteenth-century reredos with Victorian figures. The ceiling, though once painted over, is now seen much as it was six hundred years ago, and the shrine of St Alban himself has been partially and painstakingly put together. The grandest tomb in the abbey is that of Duke Humphrey of Gloucester, brother of Henry V, and there is a superb brass of the greatest of the abbots, Thomas de la Mare. He died in 1396 aged eighty-seven, having held office for forty-seven years.

St Albans has a new and later treasure, too. In 1539 the monks' chapter-house was demolished, along with the other monastic buildings. Over four hundred years later, in 1982, the Queen came to St Albans to open the new chapter-house, the first major modern building to be built next to a great medieval church. Designed by William Whitfield and built of bricks carefully chosen to blend with the abbey, it is the most ambitious addition to an Anglican cathedral since the Reformation. There are those who will not like it merely because they would rebel against anything new next to an ancient church, but the architect has followed his commission with an intuitive feeling for the great abbey church and has produced a building which stands up for itself but does not clash. It is a noble and worthy addition to the most ancient site in the history of English Christianity.

An artist's reconstruction of the abbey as it was when it was the first monastic house in England.

SOUTHWARK

The Cathedral Church of St Saviour and St Mary Overie

If there is fierce argument over whether Durham or Lincoln, or just possibly Salisbury, has the finest setting of any cathedral in England there can be no dispute over which has the least attractive surroundings. That particular grimy palm must be awarded to Southwark. No English cathedral, neither the great medieval ones nor the more recent parish-church cathedrals, has a more squalid setting. Tucked into a corner by London Bridge, below road level, hemmed in by old warehouses, overshadowed by a railway viaduct and never free from the roar of traffic, Southwark's setting is the very antithesis of what the peaceful cloistered calm of a cathedral is generally imagined to be. Conversely, no other cathedral can claim to be more 'in the world' to which it seeks to proclaim its message.

In writing about Southwark it would have been easy to relegate it to the chapter of notes on parish-church cathedrals, for it still is a parish church and the head of its Chapter is a provost and not a dean. Furthermore, it became a cathedral as recently as 1905, almost sixty years, for instance, after Manchester was so designated. Why then does Southwark merit a chapter and Manchester merely a note? The answer is that by any relative architectural standards Southwark does deserve to be listed with those other major medieval churches which became cathedrals during the nineteenth century, Ripon, St Albans and Southwell, though it is the least notable of the four.

Until the nineteenth century, when it was transferred to the diocese of Rochester, Southwark came within the diocese of Winchester. From the twelfth century the Bishops of Winchester had their London palace close by, and indeed Southwark's associations with Winchester go back much further, to the time of St Swithun himself. He established a college of priests along this stretch of the Thames' south bank during the sixth decade of the ninth century, and there was a monastery here at the time of Edward the Confessor.

No trace of that church remains, and only the merest traces of the first Norman church of St Mary Overie (over the water). St Mary's, an Augustinian house served by the Canons Regular of that order, dated from the eleventh century, but there was a disastrous fire in 1206 which destroyed virtually everything. It is from the rebuilding after that fire that the ancient parts of the present church date. By the mid-fourteenth century a new and fine Gothic church with a splendid choir and retrochoir had been built. That in turn was shortly to be severely damaged in another fire, but it too was repaired and Southwark was still an important Augustinian house when it was dissolved by Henry VIII in 1539. Then the priory church of St Mary Overie became the parish church of St Saviour, Southwark.

This church enjoyed a brief renaissance during the episcopacy of Stephen Gardiner, the last Roman Catholic Bishop of Winchester, who officiated at the marriage of Mary Tudor and Philip of Spain, but with his death and the end of the brief restoration of Roman Catholic supremacy during the English

The least lovely surroundings of any English cathedral.

Counter-Reformation, it fell into disrepair. So neglected was it, we are told, that pigs were kept in the choir.

The borough of Southwark, however, enjoyed great prosperity at the end of the sixteenth and the beginning of the seventeenth century. It was London's first theatre-land, set up beyond the jurisdiction of the City authorities who would not countenance 'vagabonds and players'. The Rose, the Swan, the Globe – all were here, the companies of Shakespeare and Burbage, of Henslowe, and (financially the most important) of Edward Alleyn. It was during this time, in 1614, that the parishioners bought the church from James I and restored it. Henslowe was buried here and so were the dramatists John Fletcher and Philip Massinger, two in a single grave. In 1607 there had been a particularly notable baptism, that of John Harvard, who crossed the Atlantic and founded the great American university. During the Civil War the neighbouring Winchester Palace was turned into a prison, and then allowed to fall into ruin, but the church survived, though it was no longer ministering to a rich and thriving parish.

By the middle of the nineteenth century, a hundred and fifty years of slow neglect had taken its

A roof boss depicting the Pelican in her Piety.

toll and many locals felt St Saviour's should be pulled down.

Their view did not prevail. In spite of the fact that the church was now fifteen feet below the level of the busy road, and overhung by a railway viaduct, extensive restoration of the choir and retrochoir began. The nave, however, was demolished and the future still seemed very bleak until a momentous decision was made. The population of London was expanding by the year, and it was felt that the case for a new diocese in South London was an unanswerable one. No other church was so well sited and Southwark was designated as the cathedral, a status

A view of the Early English retrochoir.

it assumed in 1905 when the diocese was created by Act of Parliament. To prepare for St Saviour's new dignity and responsibilities a plan for major extensions was produced. Between 1889 and 1897 the fine new nave was built. Designed by Sir Arthur Blomfield, it is one of England's most successful Victorian Gothic buildings.

Southwark's great glory, however, the feature which gives it its claim to be ranked among the important English medieval cathedrals, is its magnificent choir. With its five bays and its triple

Southwark as it was in 1840, an engraving after a drawing by Hablot Browne.

arcaded clerestory it has been described by Alec Clifton Taylor as 'purest Early English'. It is complemented by a fine retrochoir of similar date and between is a splendid early sixteenth-century reredos only slightly marred by its Victorian figures.

Two of Southwark's finest tombs are those of John Gower, the fifteenth-century poet, and of Bishop Lancelot Andrews who died in 1626. Both were restored in the 1930s by Sir Ninian Comper who was also responsible for the east window and much other work in the cathedral, including all of the furnishings for its four chapels.

Among Southwark's other treasures are a Jacobean communion table and one of the earliest wooden effigies in England, a figure of a knight which dates from the last quarter of the thirteenth century. The Harvard Chapel has been lavishly adorned as a result of the gifts of members of the university and there is a suitably prominent memorial to Bishop Talbot, who came from Rochester to be the first Bishop of Southwark in 1905.

Outside the roar of traffic never ceases. Inside there is a chance to pause and be still in an ancient monastic church which has seen more changes within and without than any other English cathedral.

The supremely beautiful Early English choir.

SOUTHWELL

The Cathedral and Parish Church of St Mary the Virgin

Though its church did not become a cathedral until 1884 when a new diocese for Nottinghamshire and Derbyshire was carved out of the archdiocese of York, Southwell, now England's smallest cathedral city (towns with cathedrals are always cities) grew up around its great church. It is a delightful, well-ordered, very clerical sort of place, much as one imagines Trollope's Barchester must have been.

Though it still serves as a parish church, and the head of its Chapter is therefore a provost rather than a dean, Southwell has all the atmosphere of a cathedral and is indeed in a very different league from those other parish-church cathedrals created to meet the demands of rising populations in the last century. It has been the mother church of Nottinghamshire since the twelfth century, overseeing part of the vast diocese of York, just as Ripon and Beverley did.

Like those two other churches Southwell bears the title minster, a lovely word of no very precise meaning which was applied to some monastic foundations and also some collegiate churches. Collegiate churches were specially important churches where the group of priests who served them were known as a College. They were secular canons who had parish responsibilities and who were financed by special endowments of land and tithes called prebends. Together they would run the affairs of their church, appointing deputies or vicars, priest and lay, to sing the offices and fulfil other duties when they were absent. In Southwell, for instance, one of these vicars had specific charge of the parish and another was master of the grammar school. The whole of the collegiate body here eventually numbered sixty, of whom forty-seven were always in residence. As the Archbishop of York also kept a palace here Southwell was, by the thirteenth century, a cathedral city in all but name.

The first archbishop whom we know to have established a church and body of clergy here was Oskytel in 956. Within a few years Southwell had become a place of pilgrimage as the church contained the shrine of St Eadburgh, one of those royal ladies of great piety who figured so largely in the history of the Saxon church.

The only remains of the earliest church are some small pieces of tessellated paving and an eleventh-century tympanum showing St Michael and the dragon, and David rescuing the lamb from the lion.

The first Norman archbishop to devote attention to Southwell was Archbishop Thomas, the second of that name, early in the twelfth century. He sent out a letter to the people of Nottinghamshire asking them to give alms for the building of the church of St Mary of Southwell, and releasing them from their obligations to York in return. The letter is still preserved here today.

It is thus fitting that Southwell should appear from the outside as such a classic example of a Norman church, with its rather curious pyramid steeples, quite unlike anything on any other English

The tympanum – probably eleventh century – which forms a lintel over the doorway in the west wall of the north transept.

The Leaves of Southwell: a detail of some of the magnificent carving around the doorway into the chapter house.

*The west front with the pyramid steeples which were
added in the nineteenth century.*

cathedral. These in fact date from the last century though they are very much in the spirit of the original Norman design. But the exterior is not exciting and the west towers and even the extraordinary round clerestory windows hardly prepare the visitor for an introduction to the magnificent Norman nave which, together with the towers and transepts, has remained virtually unaltered since the twelfth century. Southwell provides one of the very finest examples of Romanesque architecture in England, the cream Mansfield stone of the massive, boldly carved pillars with triforium and clerestory above giving a marvellously comforting lightness to the interior.

With its fine crossing and quaintly carved capitals, this is Norman work of the highest order – but it is not the principal glory of Southwell. Sometime around the beginning of the thirteenth century the east end, the first part of the Norman church to be built, was replaced by one of the best of Early English choirs, and early in the next century one of the most beautiful of Decorated pulpitums was erected. The choir and pulpitum, and Southwell's fixed canopied stalls with their fine misericords, would each place this small cathedral

on any list of the most distinguished churches in England, but for the visitor the best is yet to come: the chapter-house.

Built in the last decade of the thirteenth century, it is one of the smaller surviving chapter-houses, and though those at Wells and Lincoln and Salisbury might challenge or even surpass it in architectural elegance, there is nowhere in any English cathedral or church where we can see a greater profusion of magnificent carving. The 'Leaves of Southwell' are, in the words of Alec Clifton Taylor, 'the supreme example of middle Gothic nature worship'. With a love and knowledge of the leaves of the field, a consummate mastery of the techniques of stone carving, and a discipline that contained imagination sufficiently to produce a harmonious and perfectly balanced work of art, the carvers of Southwell immortalized the trees and hedgerows of the countryside. Here we find oak, hawthorn, apple and many others in a stunning profusion, on doorways, capitals, arches, spandrels and bosses. Among the leaves are beasts of the forests and the imagination; heads which were doubtless modelled by one mason for another; the green man of primeval folklore, and many other studies of genius and flights of fancy. They will always hold a special place in my affection for they were the first works of art to captivate me as a small boy; I was completely fascinated by their intricate beauty, though I had no idea then of their real importance.

The chapter-house was conceived and created before the pulpitum, itself one of the most accomplished of screens. Together they make Southwell worthy of a special journey. I would place them, with the Norman work at Kilpeck in Herefordshire, as the finest stone carving in England.

Mercifully, not being a monastery, Southwell survived the upheaval of the Reformation, but in the Civil War there was much destruction in the town

*The nave, looking towards
the Early English
choir.*

and the church did not escape, though it was the archbishop's palace that suffered most. It was completely destroyed.

In the long ecclesiastical twilight of the eighteenth century Southwell suffered from natural disaster. Its south-west spire was struck by lightning in 1711 and the roof of the nave and the central tower were destroyed. Towards the end of the century James Wyatt was brought in to advise on the fabric but fortunately for us he handed over the work to another. The man principally responsible for the restoration at Southwell during the early nineteenth century was a local architect, Richard Ingeleman. Local knowledge and affection must have restrained any tendency towards exuberance

he might have had, and he seemed content to exercise his architectural ingenuity in designing assembly rooms, a grammar school, and a fitting residence for the Chapter.

In the middle of the century Southwell lost its collegiate foundation, but the period of demotion was brief for in 1884 the minster church became the cathedral of a new diocese. Ewan Christian, who was responsible for much of the sensitive and successful work at Carlisle, came here and it is to him that we owe the western spires that replace those removed at the beginning of the century.

Southwell is not notable for great tombs or effigies, although the tomb of Archbishop Sandys who died in 1588, the year of the Armada, is an impressive piece of work in the famous Nottingham alabaster. There is also a splendid lectern with a romantic history. The monks of Newstead Abbey threw it into the lake there at the dissolution and a dean of Lincoln bought it from an antique dealer in 1805 and gave it to Southwell.

However, the abiding treasures of Southwell commemorate no one in particular and are fortunately not portable. They are the carvings of a group of anonymous artists, the quality of whose work was surpassed nowhere in Europe. It represents in every sense the finest flowering of the Middle Ages.

*The magnificent doorway
into the chapter-
house.*

THE MODERN CATHEDRALS

COVENTRY

The Cathedral Church of St Michael

If the visitor to Guildford has to shed some fondly held views of what a cathedral should look like, the visitor to Coventry has to cast them all aside. For this is a unique building: the only genuinely twentieth-century Anglican cathedral.

There was a cathedral here before the Reformation. The diocese of Lichfield and Coventry had two cathedrals, and although with the dissolution of the monasteries Coventry cathedral was allowed to fall into ruin, the bishops continued to style themselves 'Coventry and Lichfield' until the Restoration in 1660, when the title was changed to 'Lichfield and Coventry' because Lichfield had given more support to the royal cause during the

Christ in Majesty, the enormous tapestry by Graham Sutherland which dominates the interior.

The exterior showing Sir Jacob Epstein's statue of St Michael, one of his latest and finest works.

Civil War. And so it remained until Coventry was absorbed into the diocese of Worcester in the last century. Then in 1918 a new Coventry diocese was created. The old cathedral was long gone and so St Michael's Church became the cathedral. A noble parish church with one of the most magnificent spires in England, it was a fitting choice.

On 14 November 1940 all Coventry burned and St Michael's with it, smashed into smouldering oblivion by German bombs. On the morning after the blitz two crosses were placed in the fire-blackened ruins, one made of two charred pieces of wood from the old church roof and the other from nails found among the rubble. The clergy of Coventry determined that those crosses should symbolize reconciliation and that a new church should rise out

A view from the Chapel of Unity towards John Piper's multi-coloured baptistry window.

of the ashes of the old, preserving within its environs the glorious spire that had miraculously survived.

The first notion was to rebuild in the Gothic style, but then it was felt that Coventry's dreadful experience was so special to the twentieth century that the building to be erected ought to be a beautiful new creation arising from one of the worst of times. An architectural competition was held and the winner was Basil Spence. His cathedral, with furnishings contributed by some of the notable artists of the day, was built in six years. The foundation stone was laid by the Queen in 1956 and the building was consecrated in 1962. A sensitive attempt was made to link the past with the present and to enshrine the shattering and searing experience of November 1940, for the spire and ruins of the old church were preserved and the new was faced with stone – sandstone and green slate.

The new cathedral is set at right angles to the old, the shell of which is its forecourt. From there the visitor mounts steps to a spacious porch. Outside is Epstein's compelling figure of St Michael, one of his last and greatest works. The cathedral is entered through an enormous glass screen engraved with wraith-like figures of saints and angels. This opens into a great high hall which is divided by slender columns with a concrete vault above. The whole is dominated by Graham Sutherland's huge tapestry of Christ in Majesty which hangs behind the high altar.

It is perhaps the best thought-out and most carefully executed scheme for bringing together the works of a specific group of artists ever conceived for an English cathedral. The tapestry is challenging and, though some of the stained glass is not strikingly successful, the force of the whole idea is irresistible. And Coventry has one great glory which is surely fit to rank with England's finest cathedral treasures – the gloriously coloured and jewelled baptistry window by John Piper. This must be the most memorable stained glass made in Britain this century. For me both the baptistry and the Gethsemane chapels are triumphantly successful.

Some people will not like Coventry because it is different, but millions have come here and few can fail to be impressed by the loving care and thought that has gone into creating this building, one that excites far deeper feelings than mere approval. Here you can appreciate the worst and the best that men can do.

The new cathedral rises among

the ruins of the old.

GUILDFORD

The Cathedral of the Holy Spirit

From afar it is difficult to accept that this vast gaunt red brick building on Stag Hill, a site reminiscent of that enjoyed by Lincoln, is a cathedral, so conditioned are we to the traditional image of the Gothic stone building. And yet Guildford is in the Gothic tradition and, in its own way, a moving and successful building.

The see was created when the diocese of Winchester was divided in 1927, and because the parish church was considered far too small to be the cathedral of a major new diocese an architectural competition to design a new cathedral was held in 1932. There were eighty-three entries and the winner was Edward Maufe. Building began on Stag Hill in 1936. It was soon interrupted and most of what we see today was built between 1952 and 1965, in which year the Queen came to the consecration service of the first cathedral in the south of England to be built on a new site since Salisbury replaced Old Sarum in the thirteenth century.

The whitewashed austerity of the nave and south aisle.

The severe but basically Gothic lines of one of the most impressively sited of English cathedrals.

Outside, the red brick exterior is stark and clear but the very unfussiness and austerity is impressive. Inside, the Gothic influence on Maufe is much more apparent. The brickwork is covered with plaster and there is a magnificent feeling of spaciousness, as in the best of the great medieval cathedrals.

Unfortunately not much more can be said in enthusiastic tone. Most of the furnishings are pedestrian and uninteresting. There is no really good glass, and although the statues of the seven Christian virtues and of the Virgin and Child are inoffensive, they are uninspiring. There is an elegant baptistry with a blue vaulted ceiling and a cream marble floor, and a fine carpet before the high altar.

*The painted roof over the
east end.*

A special feature of the cathedral is the amazing array of embroidered kneelers, every one of them divided diagonally, the lower half to symbolize the hill, the upper half to suggest the sky.

One unique feature of Guildford is its guide book, for it is written by the architect himself. Sir Edward quotes his words from his competition report in 1932: 'The ideal has been to produce a design, definitely of our own time, yet in the line of the great English cathedrals, to build anew on tradition, to rely on proportion, mass, volume and line rather than on elaboration and ornament.' It would be a very prejudiced and blinkered visitor who denied that he had come close to realizing that ideal, though the lack of elaboration and ornament, commendable in itself perhaps, would have been more effective if the few embellishments allowed had been of a higher quality.

LIVERPOOL

Cathedral Church of Christ

It is very difficult not to run out of superlatives when talking about Liverpool. With Barry's Palace of Westminster, it is one of the two finest and most majestic buildings in the Gothic style erected in Britain since the Middle Ages. Its site is magnificent, its size overwhelming (it is the largest cathedral in Christendom after St Peter's in Rome), its tower dominating. There will never be anything like it built again.

Begun in 1904, it was not completed until 1978 and most people first gained some idea of its grandeur when the service to mark its completion was televised. It is another television occasion, however, which will be remembered even more vividly: the Pope's visit in 1982 when he walked from one of Liverpool's twentieth-century cathedrals to another. Charity alone restrains me from saying anything about the other, the Roman Catholic, cathedral, save that it is extraordinary.

Giles Gilbert Scott was only twenty-two when his design was selected from more than a hundred others submitted in the competition to design a fitting cathedral for the huge new Merseyside diocese. He worked on the cathedral until his death in 1960 and had it not been for the two world wars would have seen it completed. He altered his original design more than once, for the better most would say.

Although Scott worked in the Gothic style his symmetrical proportions are remarkably classical.

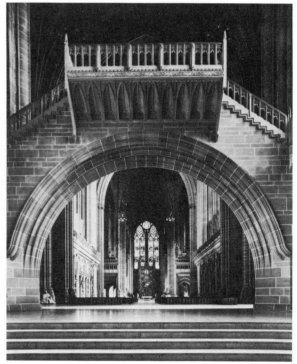

Looking east through the stone bridge towards the choir.

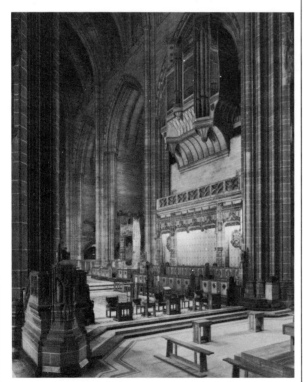

A view of the organ and choir stalls in the most magnificent of twentieth-century Gothic buildings.

The problems of height and space have been mastered with a mathematical discipline, but inspired with a soaring imagination and a deep knowledge and love of what he was doing.

The tower, 331 feet high, ranks with Barry's great Victoria tower at the Palace of Westminster. Inside there is much to excite both admiration and awe. There is a superb bridge over the nave, a great

The largest Christian cathedral in the world after
St Peter's in Rome.

canopy over the font. Always the eye is lifted up. The whole cathedral is 619 feet in length, a magnificently covered space as long as the terraced front of the Palace of Westminster – comparisons with Barry are difficult to resist, so effortlessly did both men master breadth, neither crushing nor boring visitor or worshipper.

There is much inside Liverpool that is fine too, unlike Guildford, where Maufe's design is so badly served. The organ case in English oak ranks with the best, and the reredos behind the high altar, if it does not do that, at least is no disgrace. Even the monuments already accumulated seem appropriate to a great church, especially that of Frederick, sixteenth Earl of Derby, first President of the Cathedral Committee.

There was no native modesty here in Liverpool. Not only were they to have a great and glorious cathedral but a Lady Chapel of splendour and an octagonal chapter-house too.

Of the four cathedrals built in the past hundred years Coventry may evoke the most poignant thoughts, but only Liverpool will undoubtedly be regarded a century from now as a great building in its own right, in conception and execution as well as in size.

The Lady Chapel, impressive
in both grandeur
and scale.

TRURO

The Cathedral Church of St Mary

Truro is a text-book cathedral. From afar, the unknowing visitor might think himself in Brittany or Normandy approaching one of those tall, narrow-fronted Celtic churches. The appearance is deceptive for this is a Victorian Gothic church built in the last twenty years of the nineteenth century.

Its origins alone make it a fascinating building. Though the faith came to Cornwall before St Augustine came to Canterbury and though there was a Cornish bishop in the tenth century, before William of Normandy came the see of Cornwall had already been united with that of Crediton. The united see moved to Exeter and for over eight hundred years Cornish churchmen were in the diocese of a Devon bishop. It was not until 1876 that Disraeli, more impressed by Cornwall's special character than Gladstone had been (*he* thought the penny post and the railway made a new see unnecessary), agreed to the establishment of a Cornish bishopric.

In 1877 Dr Edward White Benson came from Lincoln, where he had been Chancellor, to Truro. For seven years he administered his diocese from a wooden hut, and it was there that he devised the service of nine lessons and carols that is now such a traditional part of almost every church's English Christmas. During those seven years a new cathedral was built, for Benson would not countenance the old and dilapidated St Mary's parish church serving as centre of an important new diocese. Truro was thus the first purpose-built cathedral to be erected in a new diocese since the Middle Ages

A view of the sanctuary showing the high altar and the reredos designed by John Pearson and carved by Nathaniel Hitch.

Looking over the town towards the cathedral,
a view that is reminiscent
of Brittany.

and the only cathedral, apart from the new St Paul's, that had been built in England for some six hundred years.

The architect was John Loughborough Pearson, one of the foremost ecclesiastical architects of the day. Born in 1817, he had established his reputation with a series of splendid Gothic Revival churches and by his restoration work, less universally admired now, at Lichfield, Chichester, Peterborough, Bristol and Westminster Abbey.

The foundation stone was laid in 1880 and the cathedral finished by Pearson's son, with the erection of the spires on the west tower, in 1910. Some have dismissed Truro as a mere exercise in scholarship with nothing creative or original about it. Certainly the incorporation of one of the aisles of the old St Mary's church, with its white walls and Cornish waggon roof – an understandable gesture to local sympathies – is not entirely successful. But that apart Truro is, by any standards, an outstanding example of high Victorian art.

It is quite obvious that Pearson was greatly influenced by the cathedrals on which he had worked and by those he had admired in France as well as in England, but this is a very personal and individual building and a fitting centre for a new see.

Of particular note are the sanctuary with its elaborate reredos and marble flooring; the retrochoir, which contains three chapels and forms an ambulatory linking the north and south choir transepts and aisles; the splendidly carved and canopied stalls; and, finest of all, the magnificent series of

Victorian stained glass windows by Clayton and Bell, who were among the best of all the many firms who worked in glass in the nineteenth century.

The choir and the transepts were completed by 1887 and the nave was dedicated in 1903. Pearson died in 1897 and his son carried on his work. When the building of the cathedral was completed in 1910, its towers were dedicated to the memory of Edward VII (who as Prince of Wales had laid the foundation stone thirty years previously), and to his widow Queen Alexandra.

In 1935 the first bay of the cloisters was built but the work was interrupted by war. The cathedral was finally completed, with the addition of a modern chapter-house, in 1967. Truro is very much in the Gothic tradition in that the prime emphasis within is on the choir, where the daily offices are performed. The nave was conceived as a great church to be used only for major diocesan occasions. Pearson's skilful use of perspective makes it appear bigger than it is; in fact it is a perfect cathedral in miniature.

The John Robartes memorial,
elaborately ornamented
in the baroque style.

PARISH CHURCH CATHEDRALS

During the period between 1836 and 1927 no less than twenty new dioceses were carved out of the old ecclesiastical map of England and this meant the creation of twenty new cathedrals. As we have seen, four of them – Ripon, St Albans, Southwell and Southwark – had always been great churches, two of them abbey churches and two collegiate churches governed by colleges of canons. Four other cathedrals have been newly built in the past century. The remaining twelve are all former parish churches. No book on the cathedrals of England can be complete without a mention of them and in this final chapter the most significant and interesting features of each one are briefly outlined, for they are all well worth a visit.

There is one important point about the organization of these new cathedrals. All of them except Manchester still serve as parish churches, as do the cathedrals of Southwark, Ripon and Southwell, and because of this in each case the head of the cathedral Chapter, who is also an incumbent, is called the provost and not the dean.

A south-west view of Birmingham Cathedral, Archer's Midland masterpiece.

BIRMINGHAM

The Cathedral Church of St Philip

Birmingham is a very fine eighteenth-century church. Consecrated in 1715, it was the work of a famous local architect, Thomas Archer, who is perhaps best known for St John's, Smith Square, in London. Archer's magnificent baroque was added to in 1884 when the church was enlarged. In 1905 St Philip's was designated as the cathedral for the new and important diocese of Birmingham. Among the treasures of Birmingham's new cathedral are a series of four great windows by Edward Burne-Jones, himself a native of the city, two splendid eighteenth-century organ cases, a very fine eighteenth-century wrought iron screen at the east end and some good box pews in the nave.

Among the memorial tablets is one commemorating Peter Oliver, an American who remained loyal to George III during the War of Independence. The cathedral has recently been the subject of much careful restoration and is one of the very best examples in the country of a major eighteenth-century town church.

BLACKBURN

Cathedral and Parish Church of St Mary the Virgin

Blackburn is mainly the work of John Palmer, a pioneer of the Gothic Revival in England, and was consecrated in 1826. It became the cathedral of the new diocese of Blackburn exactly a century later, since when the original church has been considerably enlarged, in a mostly successful attempt to give it a new dignity worthy of its enhanced status.

Palmer's nave remains, with a series of magnificent early nineteenth-century roof bosses. There is a dignified bishop's throne and an exciting and successful corona over the high altar, very much in the twentieth-century idiom, as are the egg-shaped font and many of the other furnishings.

The cathedral church of Blackburn from the north. Consecrated in 1826, it was one of the first churches of the Gothic Revival.

A view looking west from Birmingham's choir, one of the finest of eighteenth-century interiors.

BRADFORD

The Cathedral and Parish Church of St Peter

Bradford illustrates at first sight the problems confronting a parish church that is suddenly, as it was in 1919, elevated in status. There is a fine fifteenth-century tower and, on either side, wings erected in the 1950s. Doubtless the facilities they provide were much needed, but the impression is as if municipal offices had been added to an isolated tower, since, from the front, they hide much of the rest of the church. In fact most of the present nave was part of the fifteenth-century church, with the clerestory, south wall and porch dating from the mid-nineteenth century, and the transepts from about fifty years later. As a further addition – and we must remember that medieval cathedrals grew as needs demanded and styles changed – a new east end was designed by Sir Edward Maufe, architect of Guildford Cathedral. Built in the 1960s, it includes an ambulatory, three chapels and a chapter-house as well as the chancel. An attempt has also been made to give Bradford a cathedral environment, with houses in a landscaped close for the provost and two of the canons.

Inside the marriage of ancient and modern is far more harmonious than outside appearances might lead the visitor to expect. Among Bradford's treasures are a fine memorial tablet by the great eighteenth-century Yorkshire sculptor John Flaxman and a group of William Morris windows in the Lady Chapel.

The choir and sanctuary at Bradford, looking towards the new east end.

Bradford Cathedral from the south-west.

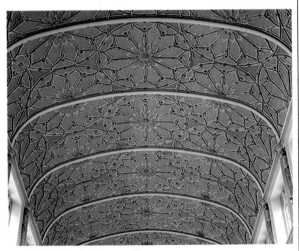

The nave roof at Chelmsford.

CHELMSFORD

The Cathedral and Parish Church of
St Mary the Virgin and St Peter and St Cedd

Essex's ancient Christian history is emphasized in the joint dedication to St Cedd, who came to these parts from Northumbria in the seventh century: a dedication that was made as recently as 1954 in this parish church which became a cathedral in 1914. Much of the ancient parish church collapsed in 1800 and so a great deal of what we see today is a result of the rebuilding which followed that disaster.

Chelmsford's great glory is its magnificent fifteenth-century tower, and the whole cathedral has recently been the subject of a major internal reorganization and restoration.

DERBY

The Cathedral and Parish Church of All Saints

Here again we have the familiar story of a parish church being too small to serve adequately as a cathedral for an important and heavily populated new diocese. All that remains of the once important medieval collegiate church is the famous tower, completed around 1530. The nave is the work of James Gibbs and dates from 1723. The spectacular retrochoir was added much more recently. The work of Sebastian Comper, it was completed in 1972. Comper's superb baldacchino blends magnificently with the work of Gibbs and must rank as one of the least incongruous and most successful modern additions to any church in the country.

Among the treasures of Derby are some magnificent monuments by Nollekens, Rysbrack and Chantrey but the most famous of all is much earlier, that to the Elizabethan Bess of Hardwick, one of the most remarkable women in English history. There is also an interesting tablet erected in 1945 to commemorate the two-hundredth anniversary of the arrival of Charles Edward, the Young Pretender, at the head of his Jacobite forces on 'Black Friday' in 1745. Derby became a cathedral in 1927.

An interior view of Derby Cathedral, looking down on the nave from the west end.

LEICESTER

The Cathedral and Parish Church of St Martin

Although St Martin's has a medieval plan, what we see is almost entirely Victorian. It has a soaring, splendid spire 220 feet high which dates from 1867 and some fine memorials in the Herrick Chapel. It became a cathedral in 1927.

There is fine eighteenth-century furniture in the medieval Lady Chapel, which now serves as the consistory court, but its most unusual feature is undoubtedly the double south aisle.

An external view of Leicester Cathedral showing its dominating spire, built in 1867.

MANCHESTER

The Cathedral and Parish Church of St Mary, St George and St Denys

Manchester is one of the oldest of the new cathedrals, having been designated as such in 1847. The building began here in 1422 of a great collegiate parish church built for a college of secular canons. The noble tower was partly rebuilt in 1867 and beneath there is some magnificent nineteenth-century fan vaulting. Another nineteenth-century addition is the Victoria porch at the foot of the tower, built to commemorate the Queen's Diamond Jubilee in 1897. There is a fine timber roof in the nave and here again there was considerable alteration in the last century, when even the superb fifteenth-century pulpitum received attention. Manchester has fine choir stalls too, and were it not for the way in which the restorers went to work it would rank with Ripon, St Albans, Southwell and Southwark, the other great medieval churches designated as cathedrals in the last century.

The choir at Manchester, looking west.

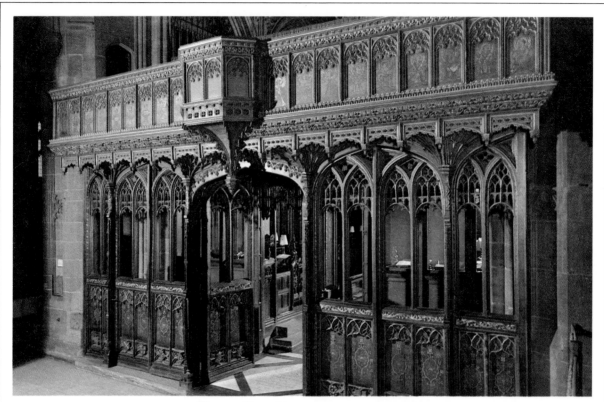

*The magnificent fifteenth-century choir screen
at Manchester.*

NEWCASTLE

Cathedral and Parish Church of St Nicholas

This is one of the very great parish churches of England, designated a cathedral in 1882. Its lantern tower is one of the most glorious of the fifteenth century, a hundred years later than most of the rest of the church. There is a fine heraldic font with a fifteenth-century canopy. The screen is nineteenth-century but worthy of its setting, as is the pulpit. Both of them were installed at the time the church became the cathedral. Of similar date is the elaborately carved reredos. Among the earlier treasures are a seventeenth-century organ case, the sixteenth-century memorial to the Maddison family, and an exquisite roundel of fourteenth-century glass showing the Virgin and Child.

Newcastle has not suffered unduly from the attention of restorers or improvers, nor was it necessary to extend the church when it attained its new status.

*The sixteenth-century Maddison memorial at Newcastle,
one of the finest of parish-
church cathedrals.*

PORTSMOUTH

The Cathedral and Parish Church of St Thomas of Canterbury

Portsmouth was carved out of the Winchester diocese at the same time as Guildford, and the church became a cathedral in 1927, since when the twelfth- and thirteenth-century sanctuary and choir, and the Jacobean tower, have been surrounded by extensions, a nave and aisle which have more than doubled the size of the church. As is to be expected in a church of one of the greatest of England's sea ports, there are many splendid naval associations here. In the new nave, for instance, there is the golden barque which served as a weather vane on the tower from 1710 to 1954. The royal arms of William and Mary (1694), carved by the master carver of the dockyard, are in the church porch. And in the south aisle of the sanctuary is the Buckingham monument, erected to commemorate George Villiers, Duke of Buckingham, favourite of

Charles I, who was assassinated by Captain Felton in the High Street in August 1628.

A particularly interesting tablet in the Navy aisle is that commemorating all the engagements in which ships called *Mary Rose* have taken part, from 1501 to 1917. A unique funeral service was held here in the summer of 1984 for all those who perished in the *Mary Rose* in 1545, and whose remains have been discovered during the recent lifting of Henry VIII's flag ship.

Indeed, because of the extraordinarily varied and fascinating history of the town, Portsmouth's cathedral, a building of no great architectural merit, is among the most fascinating of England's parish church cathedrals.

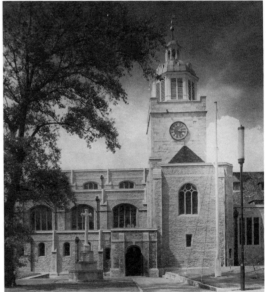

External view of Portsmouth, the naval cathedral – a parish church extended.

Looking into the choir of Portsmouth cathedral from the south aisle.

ST EDMUNDSBURY

In 1913 the parish church of St James, Bury St Edmunds, became the cathedral of the new diocese of St Edmundsbury and Ipswich. This was the heart of the great Benedictine abbey of St Edmundsbury, one of the shrines of English Christendom, founded at the place where the body of the martyred King Edmund was brought in 903.

It nearly became a cathedral twice before, once in the eleventh century, when the East Anglian see was

*A view of the nave of
St Edmundsbury
looking east.*

SHEFFIELD

The Cathedral of St Peter and St Paul

In the British Museum is the shaft of a ninth-century Saxon cross which came from Sheffield, proof that there was a place of worship on the site a thousand years before Sheffield's parish church was designated the cathedral of a new diocese in 1913. Sheffield, like most of our other parish church cathedrals, has been considerably enlarged, although in Sheffield's case the plans for a new nave were abandoned the day before building was due to begin in September 1939. Much of Sir Charles Nicholson's scheme had already been completed by then, however, and after the war though the existing nave was not, as originally planned, rebuilt it was extended and the newly enlarged cathedral was rehallowed in November 1966.

The church is a strange amalgam of Perpendicular and twentieth-century but there are some real and rare treasures here. There is a fifteenth-century

*Juxtaposition of ancient
and modern at
Sheffield.*

finally centred on Norwich, and again at the dissolution of the monasteries when Henry VIII considered making the abbey church the centre of a new diocese. But it was not to be, the abbey fell into ruin and St James's, one of the three great churches it contained, became, with St Mary's, the parish church. Not until 1913 did it attain the dignity that had twice escaped it.

This is the second church of St James to be built on the site. There have been additions during the last quarter of a century but, as with Derby, they have been sensitively and brilliantly executed, this time by Stephen Dykes Bower. There are plans for still more – tower, completed cloister, north transept – but there is already much of great distinction and beauty here, the massively impressive Norman bell tower being the cathedral's prime glory.

black oak sedile, one of only three portable ones in the country. There are fine stalls designed by Comper, a small treasury well displayed, and some magnificent tombs in what was formerly the Shrewsbury Chapel. The Talbots, Earls of Shrewsbury, held the manor of Sheffield and here George, fourth Earl of Shrewsbury, fearful that Worksop Priory would fall victim to Henry VIII, chose to be buried. He lies with his two countesses – dressed in his armour and his Garter mantle – in an unusually fine tomb. Against the south chapel is another imposing monument, to the sixth Earl, one of the husbands of Bess of Hardwick and the guardian of Mary Queen of Scots when she was imprisoned in Sheffield Castle. There is lightness and brightness here and, though it has not the aura of a great cathedral, the new and necessary functions which have come with its enhanced status have not marred what is essentially a good and historic parish church.

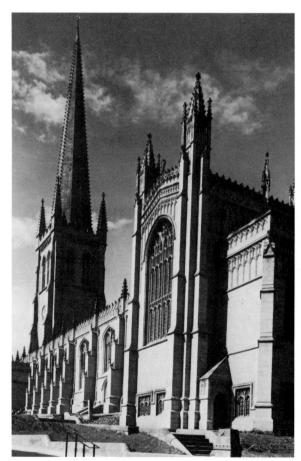

Wakefield Cathedral
from the
south-east.

WAKEFIELD

The Cathedral Church of All Saints

Here, as in so many other places, I find myself thinking of those lines by Sir John Betjeman:

> The Church's restoration in 1883
> Has left for contemplation not what there used to be.

For Wakefield medieval parish church was extensively improved and restored by Sir George Gilbert Scott and J. T. Micklethwaite before the

The screen, chancel
and retrochoir
at Wakefield.

church was raised to the status of a cathedral in 1888. Then between 1897 and 1905 it was further altered and extended by Pearson and consecrated in 1905. There is a good seventeenth-century font, and a fine memorial to Bishop Walsham Howe, the first Bishop of Wakefield. There are some excellent eighteenth-century stalls in the chancel and fine roof bosses. The rood above the screen was designed by Sir Ninian Comper and some of the glass by the Victorian, Kempe, is of high quality.

ILLUSTRATED GLOSSARY

Ambulatory The processional aisle encircling the apse.

Apse A semicircular or, sometimes, polygonal end to a church or chapel.

Arcade A range of arches which rest on piers or columns. A 'blind arcade' is one which is built on to a wall.

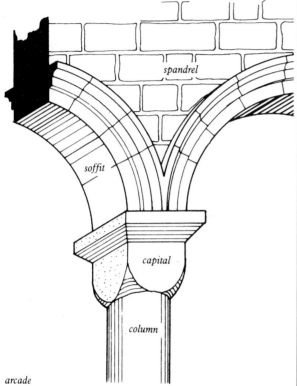

arcade

Baldacchino A large ornamental canopy over pulpit, altar etc.

Boss An ornament concealing the meeting of the ribs of a vault, usually carved with foliage or figures.

Chantry chapel A chapel within a cathedral which was originally established for the saying of masses for the soul of the departed donor.

Chapter-house The building in which those who govern the cathedral meet for their discussions, so called because a passage (or chapter) from the Bible or some religious work would be read at the meeting.

Chevron The zigzag ornamentation found on Norman pillars and arches, as at Durham.

Choir The part of the cathedral beyond the pulpitum where the services are sung.

Clerestory The line of windows above the nave, choir and transepts.

Corbel The (generally carved) stone which serves to support a roof or vault.

Corona 1 The large, flat, projecting part of a cornice which crowns the entablature; 2 a circular chandelier or hanging ornament; 3 the termination to a building.

Cornice Top section of entablature.

Crocket Projecting ornament on side of spire, pinnacle etc.

Cusp Projecting point in Gothic tracery.

Entablature Upper part of an ordered façade.

Finial Ornament terminating pinnacle, gable etc.

Galilee The name given, as at Ely or Lincoln, to a large porch which was included in the route of the Sunday procession. The name is a reference to Christ's preceding his disciples into Galilee after the Resurrection.

Gargoyle Grotesque ornamental waterspout.

Grisaille Yellow-grey medieval glass, sometimes ornamented with brown decoration.

Hammer beams Beams which project at right angles from the wall and provide support for the wooden roof.

Lady Chapel The chapel dedicated to the Blessed Virgin Mary and usually found at the east end of the church.

Lancet window A narrow window with a sharp point, characteristically Early English.

Lantern tower A tower over the crossing which projects light downwards.

Lierne vaulting Purely decorative vaulting which is characteristic of the Perpendicular period.

Misericord The underside of a wooden seat in the choir stall which gave support to those singing the services during long periods of standing, generally adorned with carvings.

Nave The main body of the church, extending eastwards from the great west door.

Pier A solid support designed to take vertical pressure.

Piscina A stone basin for washing consecrated vessels.

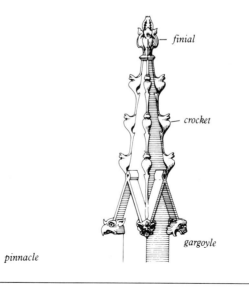

pinnacle

plate tracery

geometrical tracery

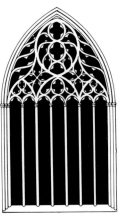

curvilinear tracery

Decorated tracery

Perpendicular tracery

Presbytery (or **Sanctuary**) The part of the cathedral east of the choir, containing the high altar.

Pulpitum The screen dividing the nave from the choir.

Pyx Receptacle in which the Eucharist Host is kept.

Retrochoir The part of the cathedral east of the presbytery and high altar.

Rood screen The screen which was normally west of the pulpit and which bore the rood, or cross.

Sedile, (pl. **Sedilia**) A priest's seat in a sanctuary, usually of stone.

Soffit The underside of an arch.

Spandrel Wall surface between two arches or on either side of arch.

Tracery The intersecting stone-work in a Gothic window or screen.

Transept One of the arms of a cruciform or cross-shaped church.

Triforium The arcaded wall passage above the main arcade of the church but below the clerestory.

Tympanum A semi circular panel, especially one within a Norman door-arch, generally filled with sculpture.

Vault Stone or wooden ceiling below roof.

Voussoir A wedge-shaped stone in an arch.

Waggon roof A curved wooden roof.

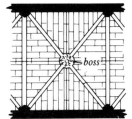

quadripartite rib vault

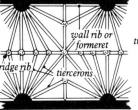

tierceron rib vault

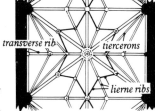

lierne vault

fan vault

BIBLIOGRAPHY

Most readers who visit cathedrals will want to buy the detailed guide books on sale there. Fortunately most of these are attractively produced and helpful, interesting and scholarly. Many are in the Pitkin *Pride of Britain* series. If, as I hope, interest in the subject has been really aroused, then among the more recent books on cathedrals, to be commended are:

John Harvey, *Cathedrals of England and Wales* (Batsford, 1974)
Alec Clifton Taylor, *Cathedrals of England* (Thames & Hudson, 1972)

Richard Morris, *Cathedrals and Abbeys of England and Wales* (Dent, 1979)
Paul Johnson, *British Cathedrals* (Weidenfeld and Nicolson, 1980)
George Dupy, *The Age of the Cathedrals* (Croom Helm, 1981).

Harvey, Morris and Johnson all have extended bibliographies, and anyone who develops a real love of the subject will find the relevant volume in Nikolaus Pevsner's regional guides *The Buildings of England* (Penguin Books) quite indispensable.

ACKNOWLEDGMENTS

The pictures in this book are reproduced by kind permission of the following:

B.T.A.: 23 left, 23 bottom, 89 right, 102
John Bethell: 12, 36, 42 right, 55, 81, 92, 117, 123, 125 left
Peter Chèze-Brown: 4, 61 top right, 65, 121 right, 139 left
Bernard Cox: 74
English Life, Derby: 143
Mary Evans: 126 top
Derek Forss: endpapers, 25, 32, 36 bottom, 44, 70, 73, 85, 90, 135
The Dean and Chapter of Lichfield Cathedral: 53
Sonia Halliday: 16, 52, 76 right, 108, 112, 113
Michael Holford: Opposite title page, 19, 38–9, 45, 60, 67 left, 77 (photo: Ethel Hurwicz), 80, 84, 103, 107, 114 right, 122 right, 128, 129 right
Angelo Hornak: 6, 18, 37 top, 72, 93, 94–5, 109, 115, 125 right
Jarrolds Colour Publications, Norwich: 104 right
Judges Ltd of Hastings: 138
A. F. Kersting: 17, 20, 21, 27 left, 28, 29, 30, 33, 34, 57, 58, 59 right, 69 left, 71, 75 top, 78, 79, 82 right, 88, 97, 99 left, 104 left, 110 left and right, 111, 116, 122 left, 124, 129 left, 131, 140, 141 right, 146 left
S. & O. Mathews: 106, 139 right
National Monuments Record: 11, 47 right, 68, 136 left

Pitkin Pictorials: 24, 98, 99 right, 136 right, 137 bottom
Rackhams of Lichfield: 54 bottom
Kenneth Scowen: 26, 46
Leon Smallwood, Ripon: 119
Edwin Smith: 22, 23 top right, 27 right, 35 left, 40, 41, 42 left, 43 left and right, 47 left, 50, 51, 56 left and right, 63, 69 right, 75 bottom, 82 left, 83 left and right, 86 left and right, 96 left and right, 100, 105 left and right, 120 left and right, 121 left, 126 bottom, 127 right, 130 left and right, 134 left and right, 141 right, 146 right, 147 left and right, 148 right.
Patrick Thurston: 114 left, 132–3
Trinity College, Cambridge: 9
Victoria and Albert Museum: 76 left
Derek Widdicombe: 31, 35 right
Andy Williams: 62, 137 top
Woodmansterne: 48, 49, 54 top, 59 left, 64 left and right, 67 right, 89 left, 91, 142 top left – photos: Clive Friend 61 bottom, 66, 87, 101, 118, 127 left, 142 right, 142 bottom, 144 right, 145 top – photos: Nicolas Servian 144 left, 145 bottom, 148 left – photos: Jeremy Marks

For the drawings on pages 15, 149 and 150 the publishers would like to thank John J. Sambrook. They first appeared in James Stevens Curl's *English Architecture: an Illustrated Glossary*.

INDEX

INDEX